Tax Facts 15

Tax Facts 15

Milagros Palacios, Niels Veldhuis & Michael Walker

FRASER INSTITUTE

The Fraser Institute
www.fraserinstitute.org
2008

The authors of this book have worked independently and opinions expressed by them are, therefore, their own, and do not necessarily reflect the opinions of the supporters, trustees, or staff of the Fraser Institute. This publication in no way implies that the Fraser Institute, its trustees, or staff are in favour of, or oppose the passage of, any bill.

Editing, design, and production by Lindsey Thomas Martin
Cover design by Bill Ray
Image for front cover: ©2008 Bill Ray

Date of issue: April 2008
Printed and bound in Canada

National Library of Canada Cataloguing in Publication Data

Palacios, Milagros, 1974–
Tax facts 15 / by Milagros Palacios, Niels Veldhuis, and Michael Walker.

Includes bibliographical references.
ISBN 978-088975-231-3

1. Taxation--Canada. 2. Tax incidence--Canada. I. Walker, Michael, 1945– II. Veldhuis, Niels, 1977– III. Title. IV. Title: Tax facts fifteen.

HJ2449.V44 2008 336.2'00971 C2008-910802-2

Contents

Tables

Figures

About the Authors

MILAGROS PALACIOS is a Senior Research Economist in the Fiscal Studies Department at the Fraser Institute. She holds a Bachelors degree in Industrial Engineering from the Pontifical Catholic University of Peru and an M.Sc. in Economics from the University of Concepción, Chile. She is co-author of the *Measuring Labour Markets in Canada and the United States* (2007), *Fiscal Performance Index* (2007), *Tax Freedom Day* (2007), *Canadian Provincial Investment Climate Report* (2007), *An Empirical Comparison of Labour Relations Laws in Canada and the United States* (2006), *Union Disclosure in Canada and the United States* (2006), *Canadian Government Debt* (2006), and *Transparency of Labour Relations Boards in Canada and the United States* (2005). Her recent commentaries have appeared in such newspapers as the *National Post* and *Windsor Star*. Since joining the Institute, Ms. Palacios has written regularly for *Fraser Forum* on a wide range of topics including labour regulation, fiscal issues, taxation, charitable giving, and a host of environmental issues such as air quality, Kyoto, and water transfers.

NIELS VELDHUIS is Director of Fiscal Studies at the Fraser Institute. Since joining the Institute in 2002, he has authored or co-authored three books and 29 comprehensive studies on a wide range of topics including taxation, productivity, entrepreneurship, labor markets, and government failure. Mr. Veldhuis has written over 100 articles, which have appeared in over 40 newspapers including the *National Post*, *Globe & Mail*, and *Wall Street Journal*. He appears regularly on radio and television programs across the country and has appeared before committees of both the House of Commons and the Senate as an expert witness. Mr. Veldhuis received a Bachelor degree in Business Administration, with joint majors in business and economics, and a Master Degree in Economics from Simon Fraser University.

MICHAEL WALKER is a Senior Fellow at the Fraser Institute and President of the Fraser Institute Foundation. From its inception in 1974 until September 2005, Michael Walker directed the activities of the Fraser Institute. Before that he taught at the University of Western Ontario and Carleton and was employed at the Bank of Canada and the Federal Department of

Finance. He received his Ph.D. at the University of Western Ontario and his B.A. at St. Francis Xavier University. As an economist, he has written or edited 50 books on economic topics. His articles on technical economic subjects have appeared in professional journals in Canada, the United States and Europe, including the *Canadian Journal of Economics*, the *American Economic Review*, the *Journal of Finance*, the *Canadian Tax Journal*, *Health Management Quarterly*, and *Health Affairs*.

As a journalist, he has written some 700 articles that have appeared in some 60 newspapers, including the *Globe and Mail*, the *Wall Street Journal*, the *National Post*, the *Vancouver Sun*, the *Chicago Tribune*, the *Reader's Digest*, the *Detroit News*, and the *Western Star*—the latter being the newspaper in his birthplace, Corner Brook, Newfoundland. As a broadcaster, he has written and delivered some 2,000 radio broadcasts on economic topics and appeared on radio and television programmes in Canada, the United States and Latin America. As a consultant, he has provided advice to private groups and governments in the United States, Argentina, Australia, Bermuda, Brazil, Chile, Germany, Hong Kong, Iceland, Jamaica, New Zealand, Mexico, Panama, Peru, Sweden, Venezuela and Canada. He has lectured to over 2,000 audiences at universities and in other venues on five continents.

Michael Walker is a director of a number of firms and other enterprises, including Mancal Corporation, Canaccord Capital Corporation, and The Milton and Rose D. Friedman Foundation. He is Chairman of The Pacific Academy for Advanced Studies and is on the *Financial Post* Board of Economists. In 1992, he was awarded the Colin M. Brown Freedom Medal and Award by the National Citizens' Coalition. In 2003, he received an honorary Doctor of Laws degree (LL.D.) from The University of Western Ontario. In 2004, he received The Thomas Jefferson Award from the Association of Private Enterprise Education.

Acknowledgments

We would first like to express our thanks to Kumi Harischandra for her research assistance during the course of this project. We are also pleased to acknowledge the assistance of Statistics Canada, which provided certain unpublished background data essential to this study. The Canadian Tax Simulator computer programs were originally written by David Gill, whose unsparing efforts we are pleased to acknowledge.

The sixth and seventh editions of *Tax Facts* were computed on a set of programs modified to run on a microcomputer system. These modifications were completed by Douglas T. Wills. The eighth, ninth, and tenth editions were computed using the SPSS statistical package with programming provided by Filip Palda and Isabella Horry. The eleventh, twelfth, thirteenth, and fourteenth editions were computed using Statistics Canada's Social Policy Simulation Database and Model (SPSD/M) and the SPSS statistical package. SPSD/M programming was provided by Joel Emes (11th & 12th editions) and Niels Veldhuis (13th & 14th editions). SPSS programming was provided by Joel Emes and Niels Veldhuis using the framework established by Filip Palda and Isabella Horry.

The authors would like to express their gratitude to all those involved in the production and release of this book. The authors, of course, take full and complete responsibility for any remaining errors or omissions.

Disclaimer

A portion of this analysis is based on Statistics Canada's Social Policy Simulation Database and Model (SPSD/M). The assumptions and calculations underlying the simulation results were prepared by the authors and the responsibility for the use and interpretation of these data is entirely theirs.

Preface

THIS BOOK IS A SUMMARY OF THE LATEST RESULTS of a Fraser Institute project that began in July, 1975. Its objective was to find out how much tax, in all forms, Canadians pay to federal, provincial, and municipal governments and how the size of this tax bill has changed over the years since 1961. In the interim, 14 editions of this book have been published.

The book has been written with two distinct purposes in mind: first, to provide a non-technical do-it-yourself manual so that the average Canadian family can estimate how much tax it pays; and second, to update a statistic, first published in 1976, that we call the Canadian Consumer Tax Index. This index measures how much the tax bill of an average Canadian family has increased since 1961 and by how much it is changing currently. In other words, it measures changes in the price that Canadians pay for government.

This book does not attempt to look at the benefits that Canadians receive from government in return for their taxes. Rather, it looks at the price that is paid for a product—government. It has nothing to say about the quality of the product, how much of it each of us receives, or whether we get our money's worth. These questions are, however, considered in various publications of the Fraser Institute, including *Government Spending Facts 2*, and our government report cards.

Many of the recent statistics contained in this book are based on output from Statistics Canada's Social Policy Simulation Database and Model (SPSD/M), a microsimulation model of the Canadian tax and transfer system. Prior to 1992, the analysis was done with group average data pre-compiled by Statistics Canada. Because the analysis is now built up from families, it is possible to examine the situation of particular types of taxpayers with a good deal more precision.

The Fraser Institute's calculations of the tax burden are part of an on-going program of research. In making these results available to the public we seek both to inform and to be informed. Readers who disagree with our methods or conclusions are invited to write to <info@fraserinstitute.org> to convey the nature of their reservations. In this way, our methods and our estimates can be refined and perfected.

Michael A. Walker

Tax Facts 15

Chapter 1
The Canadian Tax System

UNDOUBTEDLY, ONE OF THE MOST UNPOPULAR POLICIES in Canadian history was the introduction of the Goods and Services Tax (GST) in 1991. In part, its political unpopularity was due to the fact that many Canadians thought that this was a new tax that would increase the tax burden. But, it also reflected a deep-seated concern on the part of citizens about the process of government and revealed the belief held by many that the government was collecting too many tax dollars while accomplishing too little in the way of public services.

The most significant revelation in the reaction to the GST, however, was that the Canadian public has very little real information about the tax system. Very few knew that the GST was replacing a tax already in place and fewer still realized that the federal government's main ambition was not to raise more revenue but rather to replace the Manufacturers' Tax. Everyone who had studied the Manufacturers' Tax had concluded that it was a terrible tax that had many unintended negative effects. It was a tax that needed to be replaced but Canadians' ignorance about it was a significant barrier to its removal. While some would say that there is no such thing as a good tax, it is the case that, as long as there is a demand for public expenditures, there will have to be taxes to finance them. We now know that taxes distort people's decisions, leaving opportunities for mutually beneficial exchanges unexploited. The task, then, is to design an efficient set of taxes, one that does not unduly interfere with the types of decisions people make in the marketplace.

There is, then, something worse than a tax and that is a badly designed tax, which, in addition to taking spending power from the private sector, also distorts everyday decisions in a way that is neither desirable nor necessary. As free international trade becomes a reality, it is increasingly important that governments implement efficient and sensibly designed tax systems. A prerequisite to being able to discuss and design such taxes is a base of information about them. The purpose of this book is to provide a basic tool kit of knowledge about taxation in Canada in order to enhance the opportunity for rational debate about these issues.

This book is an important resource for everyone concerned about the extent and relatively rapid growth of taxation in this country. Between 1981 and 2007, the total tax bill of the average Canadian family from all three levels of government increased in real terms by $8,163 in 2007 dollars. Figure 1.1 charts the progress of taxes for selected years since 1981.

The many faces of the tax collector

The Canadian tax system is continually changing. To understand current developments it is important to know how the Canadian taxation system has evolved. Under the Canadian Constitution, the federal and provincial governments are essentially given unlimited powers of taxation. Under the

Figure 1.1: Federal, provincial, and municipal taxes collected from the average Canadian family, 1981–2007 ($2007)

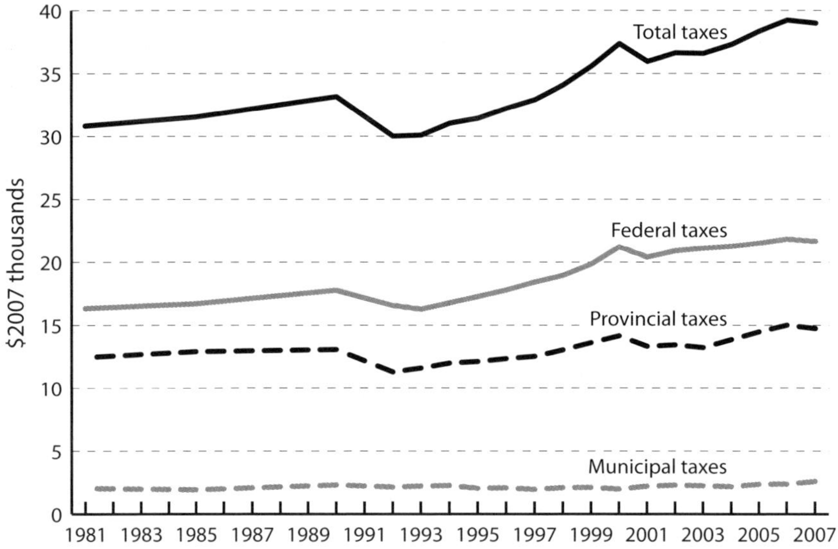

Source: The Fraser Institute's Canadian Tax Simulator 2007

British North America Act, the immediate predecessor of the Canadian Constitution, the federal parliament has the power to raise money by any mode or system of taxation while the provinces are limited to collecting taxes that are paid directly by the person being taxed—so-called direct taxes. But, because of the broad judicial interpretation of the meaning of the word "direct," the provinces have been able to levy all sorts of taxes, except for import duties and taxes on sales that cross provincial borders. Given this unlimited scope for taxation and more than 125 years of ingenuity, it is not surprising that Canada now has a very complicated tax system. See Lewis (1978), J. Harvey Perry (1989) and David B. Perry (1997) for further information on the Canadian tax system's evolution.

Income taxes predominate

Table 1.1 and figures 1.2 and 1.3 show that personal income taxes are the largest single source of government revenue. During 2006, some $181 billion was extracted by federal and provincial income tax—34.7% of the total taxes that Canadians pay. Second as a source of federal and provincial revenues was health and social service levies—16.8% of tax revenue and $87

Table 1.1: Taxes paid and percentage of total taxes, 1961 and 2006

	1961		2006	
	$millions	percent	$millions	percent
Personal income taxes	2,099	22.7	180,757	34.7
General sales taxes	1,351	14.6	68,538	13.1
Health & social insurance levies	663	7.2	87,354	16.8
Property & related taxes	1,435	15.5	51,417	9.9
Corporate income taxes	1,199	13.0	57,859	11.1
Liquor, tobacco, & amusement taxes	837	9.1	20,039	3.8
Motive fuel taxes	525	5.7	13,252	2.5
Miscellaneous taxes	55	0.6	5,192	1.0
Natural resource taxes & royalties	266	2.9	21,256	4.1
Privileges, licenses & permits	190	2.1	3,394	0.7
Customs duties	438	4.7	3,606	0.7
Other consumption taxes	173	1.9	1,864	0.4
Non-resident taxes	—	—	6,907	1.3
Total	9,231		521,435	

Sources: Statistics Canada, Public Institutions Division, cats. 68-211, 68-204, 68-207, 68-213; *National Economic and Financial Accounts*, Cat. 13-001-XPB; calculations by the authors.

Figure 1.2: Where government obtained its revenue, 1961

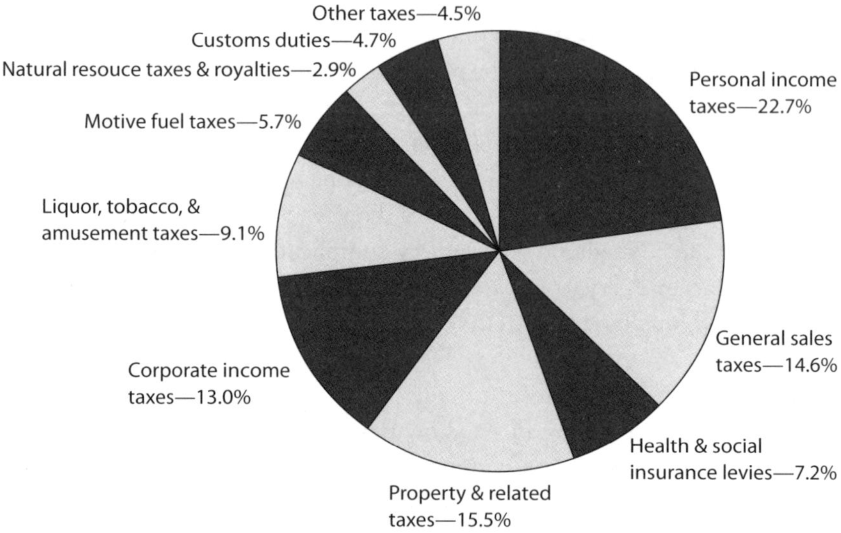

Figure 1.3: Where government obtained its revenue, 2006

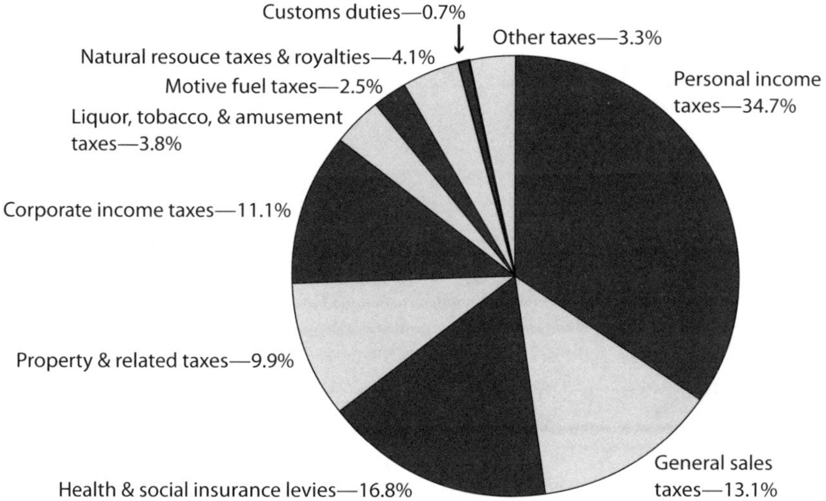

Source: Table 1.1.

billion in taxes. Sales taxes, the third largest source accounted for 13.1% of tax revenue and $68 billion in taxes. Taxes on corporate profits—11.1% of total taxes—accounted for a further $57.8 billion, while taxes on property and natural resources accounted for $72.7 billion, or 13.9%. In 2006, 45.8% of government tax revenue came from personal income tax and the tax on corporate profits, which were implemented in 1916 and 1917 as "temporary" measures to finance World War I.

Table 1.1 also illustrates how the Canadian tax structure has evolved over the 45 years between 1961 and 2006. The most obvious change has been the increased reliance on the personal income tax. While always a prominent feature of the tax system, the income tax has become even more important in the past 40 years. In 1961, income taxes represented only 22.7¢ out of every tax dollar Canadians paid but by 2006 income taxes accounted for 34.7¢—more than twice the revenue generated by the next largest source, health and social insurance taxes.

This increase came about largely through passive interaction between the progressive income-tax system and money incomes swollen by inflation. This interaction is often referred to as "bracket creep" because taxpayers can be pushed into higher tax brackets when their income goes up to compensate them for an increase in the general price level. Until the income-tax system was indexed to the inflation rate in 1974, all income increases were taxed at progressively higher rates in spite of the fact that much of the increased income represented illusory inflation-based gains. From 1974 to 1985, brackets and exemptions were increased by an "indexing factor" based on the consumer price index. From 1986 to 2000, the income-tax system was only partially indexed because the indexing factor was set at the amount by which the inflation rate exceeded 3.0%. Partial indexing meant that, although the inflation rate was 5.6% in 1991, personal income-tax exemptions and brackets increased by only 2.6% between 1991 and 1992. Exemptions and brackets stayed at their 1992 level until 1998 because inflation has been below 3.0% in every year since 1992. The Organisation for Economic Co-operation and Development (OECD) estimates that between 1988 and 1998, 18% of tax filers were pushed into a higher tax bracket because of partial indexation. In other words, 1.4 million Canadians became taxable because inflation adjustments were made to their incomes but not to their exemptions. Another 1.9 million taxpayers jumped from the 17% to 26% bracket and 0.6 million moved from the 26% to the 29% bracket. The 1998 and 1999 federal budgets increased the amount of money that could be earned before income tax applied and the 2000 federal budget brought back full indexation to the personal income-tax system.

As a consequence of this growth in revenue from personal income taxes, government was able to rely less on other forms of taxation and to allow the burden of some of these taxes to fall. However, in some important cases—notably sales tax and health and social insurance levies—the rate of tax was increased despite rapidly growing revenues from personal income tax. Table 1.2 presents the share of GDP that the top nine taxes represent.

Sales taxes

While revenue from income tax poured into the federal government's coffers, the provinces were prompted by their desire for additional tax revenue to boost their sales-tax rates. Three general exceptions are Alberta, which has no sales tax, and British Columbia and Saskatchewan, where the sales tax has been adjusted up and down. In British Columbia, the provincial sales tax was reduced from 7% in 1978 to 4% in 1979. Over the course of the following several years the sales-tax rate changed numerous times, increasing to 6% in 1981 and 7% in 1983 before being reduced to 6% in 1987. British Columbia's sales tax was again increased to 7% in 1993 and 7.5% in 2002 before being reduced back to 7.0% in 2004. In Saskatchewan, the provincial sales-tax rate was reduced to 7% from 9% in 1997 and further reduced to 6% in 1999. In 2004, the sales tax rate was raised back to 7% before being reduced to 5% in 2006.

Table 1.2: Total taxes as a percentage of Gross Domestic Product, 1961 and 2006

	1961 (%)	2006 (%)
Personal income taxes	5.1	12.5
General sales taxes	3.3	4.7
Health & social insurance levies	1.6	6.0
Property & related taxes	3.5	3.6
Corporate income taxes	2.9	4.0
Liquor, tobacco, & amusement taxes	2.0	1.4
Customs duties	1.1	0.2
Motive fuel taxes	1.3	0.9
Natural resources & other taxes	1.7	2.7
Total	22.5	36.1

Sources: Statistics Canada, *Canadian Economic Observer*, cat. 11-010 and Public Institutions Division, cats. 68-211, 68-204, 68-207, 68-213; *National Economic and Financial Accounts*, Cat. 13-001-XPB; calculations by the authors.

The federal government also sought to increase its revenue from indirect sources in the early and mid-1980s by increasing its takings from the Manufacturers' Sales Tax (MST). On January 1, 1991, the 7% Goods and Services Tax (GST) came into effect in Canada, replacing the out-dated 13.5% Manufacturers' Sales Tax, which had been in effect since 1924. The Department of Finance hoped to raise an extra $10 billion annually from this new source. Recently however, the federal government has reduced its reliance on the GST by decreasing the rate to 5% in 2008 from 6% in 2006 and 7% previously.

Taxes on natural resources

The rise in resource taxation in the 1970s and 1980s resulted primarily from increases in the price of oil and gas, triggered by the oil embargo and subsequent cartelization of oil pricing by the OPEC countries in 1973. In the normal course of events, these increases in price in Canada would automatically have meant a sharp rise in the return to Canadian producers. But, the provincial governments absorbed much of this so-called "windfall" or "rent" in the form of higher taxes or royalties. The federal government, for its part, imposed a further tax on producers who were exporting oil. This tax, the oil export charge, amounted to the difference between the controlled Canadian price per barrel and the world price. Proceeds from the federal tax were then used to subsidize imports of foreign oil into the eastern provinces. From 1974 to 1984, provincial governments and, especially, the federal government escalated their taxation of natural resources. The National Energy Program and the subsequent Energy Agreement allowed the federal government to earn about $4 billion from petroleum during 1984.

The 1985 federal budget incorporated a number of changes to energy taxes as agreed upon in the Western Accord with the governments of Saskatchewan, Alberta, and British Columbia. Both the oil-export charge and the petroleum-compensation charge were eliminated. Other energy taxes, such as the Petroleum and Gas Revenue Tax, were revised, reduced and, in some cases, phased out (Watkins and Walker, 1977, 1981; Perry, 1997: ch. 8). These changes, combined with the decline in world oil prices, resulted in a decline in energy-related revenues in both relative and absolute terms. The recent increase in oil and gas prices is responsible for the relative and absolute increase in natural resource tax revenue from natural resources.[1]

1 ◆ Effective January 2009 Alberta will increase royalty rates on oil sands, conventional oil, and natural gas.

More efficient taxation

The late 1980s and early 1990s saw the federal government trying to make income, corporate, and sales taxes more efficient and less of a burden to Canadians competing in the international marketplace. While corporate and income tax rates fell, many deductions were eliminated in order to expand the tax base. These changes were supposed to diminish the degree to which taxes enter into Canadians' decisions. If this principle seems strange, consider a flat tax. The rate of such a tax is not related to any economic activity in which the individual may engage. Government simply takes a fixed proportion of total income no matter how it is earned. The amount that the government takes may be huge but, since the tax is not related to how much an individual works or spends, it will not directly affect decisions between, for example, spending and saving or working and not working. Moreover, since the taxation rate is the same regardless of income, there is no tax disincentive to discourage an effort to move to higher income levels from any given starting income.[2]

Lowering tax rates, however, did not lead to less tax being collected: in the past 20 years, due to the expanding tax base and, more recently, to bracket creep, federal collections from the average family have risen by $4,535 in 2007 dollars. That the federal government has not collected even more taxes is due to its declining commitment to provincial projects such as welfare, education, and health care. In reaction, the provinces have made up the shortfall not by reducing spending but by increasing taxes. Since 1987, provincial collections from the average family have increased by $1,766 in 2007 dollars.

Dividing the spoils

How is total tax revenue divided among different levels of government? Tables 1.3a and 1.3b provides a breakdown of major taxes by federal, provincial, and municipal levels of government for the years 1961 and 2006. Total taxes collected now amount to 36.1¢ out of every dollar of GDP, a 60.2% rise since 1961 (see table 1.2).

These figures give a somewhat distorted impression about which level of government is doing the taxing because some municipal and provincial government revenue comes from other levels of government. For example,

2 ◆ Rabushka and Veldhuis proposed a 15% federal flat tax that would raise the same income-tax revenue raised by Canadian governments in 2006. For more information, see Clemens 2008.

Table 1.3a: Taxes collected by federal, provincial and municipal governments ($billions)

	Federal		Provincial		Municipal	
	1961	2006	1961	2006	1961	2006
Personal income taxes	2.0	110.3	0.1	70.5	0.0	0.0
Corporate income taxes	0.2	37.9	1.0	19.9	0.0	0.0
General sales taxes	0.3	33.2	1.0	35.2	0.0	0.1
Property & related taxes	0.0	0.0	0.0	9.9	1.3	41.6
Health & social insurance levies	0.5	62.3	0.2	25.1	0.0	0.0
Natural resource revenues	0.0	0.7	0.3	20.6	0.0	0.0
Customs duties	0.5	3.6	0.0	0.0	0.0	0.0
Other taxes	0.6	17.2	1.1	32.7	0.1	0.8
Total	4.1	265.1	3.7	213.9	1.4	42.4

Table 1.3b: Taxes collected by federal, provincial and municipal governments (% of total)

	Federal		Provincial		Municipal	
	1961	2006	1961	2006	1961	2006
Personal income taxes	95.2	61.0	4.8	39.0	0.0	0.0
Corporate income taxes	16.7	65.5	83.3	34.5	0.0	0.0
General sales taxes	23.1	48.5	76.9	51.4	0.0	0.1
Property & related taxes	0.0	0.0	0.0	19.2	100.0	80.8
Health & social insurance levies	71.4	71.3	28.6	28.7	0.0	0.0
Natural resource revenues	0.0	3.2	100.0	96.8	0.0	0.0
Customs duties	100.0	100.0	0.0	0.0	0.0	0.0
Other taxes	33.3	34.0	61.1	64.5	5.6	1.5
Total	44.6	50.8	40.2	41.0	15.2	8.1

Sources: Statistics Canada, Public Institutions Division, cats. 68-211, 68-204, 68-207, 68-213; *National Economic and Financial Accounts*, Cat. 13-001-XPB; calculations by the authors.

in 1961, 30% of provincial and municipal revenues were derived from other levels of government. Provinces received transfers from the federal government while municipalities received transfers from both levels. In the case of provincial revenues, the figures for 1961 reflect the tax agreement that was in effect between the federal and provincial governments. Under the agreement, the federal government rented the provinces' rights to tax personal incomes: in effect, the provinces relinquished their right to tax personal incomes in return for cash payments from the federal government, which collected all the taxes. Accordingly, the tax-collection statistics for 1961 do not reflect the division of the revenues produced but only which level of government actually collected them.

For 2006, the collection figures match the revenue as it was divided between federal and provincial governments more closely because revenue-sharing agreements have been gradually modified to eliminate tax-rental arrangements and shared-cost programs. In the years following 1978, the provinces have had, increasingly, to find their own revenues. As a consequence, tax receipts from different levels of government reflect the actual sharing of tax revenues more closely. To a considerable degree, this evolution reflects the changing attitudes of the partners in Canadian confederation: changing tax arrangements may be the first steps towards a more decentralized federation. For the 2006/07 fiscal year, Alberta received about 13.7% of its revenue from the federal government. This gives Alberta considerably more flexibility in deciding whether or not to participate in new or ongoing federal programs than, for example, Newfoundland, which receives about 40.8% of its revenue from federal sources.

The relationship between provincial and municipal government revenues reflects a different process. Municipalities now collect much less of their total revenue in the form of taxes than they did in 1961: fully 41.7% of municipal revenue is now accounted for by transfers from federal and provincial governments, mainly the latter. In large part, the emerging role of municipalities as dependencies of the provincial governments is a result of decreasing reliance on property taxation as a form of finance (see table 1.1; figures 1.2 and 1.3). Property taxes accounted for only 9.9% of total taxes in 2006, down from 15.5% in 1961.

Hidden taxation

Most people are aware of the prominent direct taxes that they pay: income tax and property tax. Many others correctly regard contributions by employees and employers to the Employment Insurance fund and the Canada and Quebec Pension Plans as taxes. Moreover, many people know how much of these taxes they pay as the information is provided on pay stubs, (e.g. income tax and contributions to EI and CPP/QPP) and annual property-tax assessments. There is, however, another class of taxes of which Canadians, by and large, are unaware. These taxes are built into the price of goods and services and are often not identified to the final consumer as a tax. These are known as "indirect" or "hidden" taxes.

Indirect taxes

The most well known of the indirect taxes are import duties, the excise taxes on items such as tobacco and alcohol, and the federal Goods and Services Tax (GST). GST legislation requires sellers to make it clear to purchasers whether the GST is included in the listed price or if it will be added when the sale is totalled. Although consumers are made aware of the tax because of this requirement, few will have a good idea of the total amount of GST they pay in a year. Other, less familiar, indirect taxes are levied on many common products. The excise taxes on such items as tobacco, alcohol, and gasoline are good examples. See figures 1.4 and 1.5 for a break-down of taxes paid for a bottle of liquor and for a litre of gasoline . Table 1.4 shows the province-by-province break-down of the pump price of gasoline. In the case of liquor, the federal rate of indirect tax is 112%. In addition, alcohol bears the provincial government's mark-up as well as a provincial sales tax. The final delivered price of alcohol is 533% above the price received by the distiller. The taxes

Figure 1.4: Typical government take from a bottle of liquor

Source: Association of Canadian Distillers. *2006 Annual Statistical Report.*

Figure 1.5: Government take from a litre of gasoline (Canadian average in cents/litre)

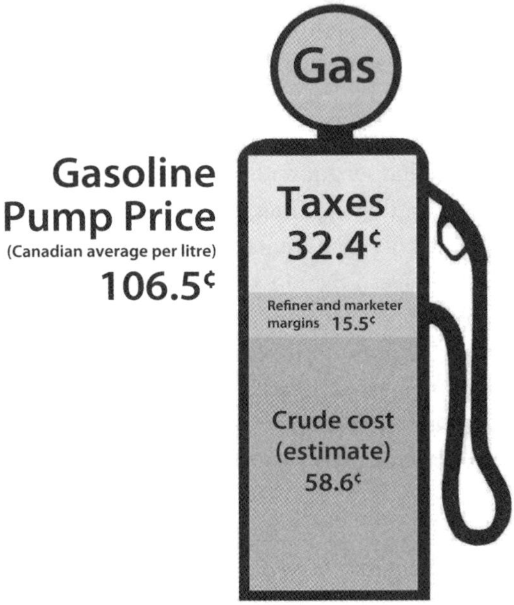

Source: Natural Resources Canada (2008, January 18). *Fuel Focus* 3, 1.

Table 1.4: Components of the price of gasoline (in cents/litre for regular unleaded gasoline at self-serve pumps), by city

	Crude cost (estimate)	Refining and marketing costs and margins	Taxes	Price at pump
Vancouver	58.6	13.2	36.1	107.9
Calgary	58.6	16.9	24.2	99.7
Regina	58.6	18.2	30.6	107.4
Winnipeg	58.6	19.4	27.0	105.0
Toronto	58.6	14.5	30.1	103.2
Montreal*	58.6	15.5	40.2	114.3
Saint John*	58.6	16.1	33.5	108.2
Halifax*	58.6	16.5	39.0	114.1
Charlottetown*	58.6	18.0	31.4	108.0
St. John's*	58.6	17.4	40.3	116.3
Canadian average	58.6	15.5	32.4	106.5

Note*: regulated markets.
Source: Natural Resources Canada (2008, January 18). *Fuel Focus* 3, 1.

on tobacco were so high that they led to widespread smuggling and tax evasion until 1994 when taxes were sharply reduced east of the Manitoba border; the western provinces stepped up enforcement instead of cutting taxes. Smuggling had become so bad that, as Ontario's finance minister at the time put it, "[i]t reached a point where the retail market in cigarettes in Ontario was in complete shambles" (McInnes 1996: A1, A4). However, in 2002 the federal government and every provincial government increased tobacco taxes. Most consumers of these products are aware that gasoline, alcohol, and tobacco are highly taxed but rarely do they know the actual rate of tax or the amount of tax that they are paying.

During 2006, total indirect taxes of all kinds amounted to $107 billion in Canada. This was 7.4% of total Canadian income and accounted for 20.6% of total government revenue from taxation. In other words, quite apart from the tax they pay when they receive their incomes, Canadians pay, on average, a further 7.4% in indirect taxes when they spend their income.

The hot potatoes—passing tax forward

Hidden taxes are hard to calculate because people try to pass them on to others—any tax that can be avoided is money in one's own pocket. As a result, throughout the economy people are constantly avoiding situations in which they will have to pay taxes and seeking to pay as little tax as possible when they cannot avoid them. The moonlighting tradesperson who engages in "cash only" transactions, the mechanic who fixes his neighbour's truck in return for free cartage, the dentist who fixes the teeth of a fellow dentist's family on a reciprocal basis, the tycoon whose business is incorporated in the Turks and Caicos Islands, all want to avoid taxes. In the end, though, when a tax is levied, somebody ends up paying. One of the most difficult and important questions in economics is to discover who that somebody is; this is known as the study of "tax incidence."

How employees pass the tax on

To get an idea of the difficulties involved, consider the following. The average Canadian employee measures his welfare in terms of after-tax dollars and in each new wage contract bargains for an increase in take-home pay. The fact that an increase in gross terms will imply a smaller increase in after-tax dollars motivates the employee or his union representative to demand a larger gross increase. By doing so, the employee is attempting to get the employer to bear the burden of the additional tax. For an example of this process, see table 1.5.

Table 1.5: Take-home pay compared to gross pay

In 2007, a single person in Ontario with an income of $35,000 had to receive a 5.6% raise in pay to realize a 5.0% increase in after-tax pay. Comparable figures for the other provinces are presented below.

NL	PE	NS	NB	QC	ON	MB	SK	AB	BC
6.0%	5.9%	6.0%	5.9%	6.4%	5.7%	5.8%	5.6%	5.7%	5.7%

Sources: Canadian Tax Foundation, *Finances of the Nation 2007*; calculations by the authors.

The employee who bargains in this manner is attempting to pass the tax forward. This behaviour is not unique; it is a general characteristic of all participants in the Canadian economy. Corporations attempt to pass the higher taxes on profits and payroll forward to the consumer in the form of higher prices or backward to employees in the form of lower wages. The difficulty in measuring the degree to which these attempts are or are not successful greatly complicates the study of tax incidence.

Who pays the indirect taxes?

While it is difficult to know where the burden of these taxes ultimately lies, it is not impossible. We need to make intelligent assumptions about how each tax is passed on. For example, a general sales tax is collected and remitted to government by retailers. It is clear, however, that in most cases the retailers do not actually bear the tax—they are merely the agents for collecting it. The actual effect of the tax is to increase the price of all goods and services affected by the tax and to cause a corresponding reduction in the purchasing power of family incomes. Accordingly, to the extent that a general sales tax causes an increase in the general level of prices, the tax is borne not by the collectors but by income earners in the economy, whose incomes now buy less. Indirect or sales taxes, therefore, burden all income earned in the economy.

Payroll taxes such as Employment Insurance premiums and contributions to the Canada and Quebec Pension Plans are collected, in part, from the employer and, in part, from the employee. And, while no one would dispute that the employee pays the employee's portion, in most cases it is true that the employee also pays the so-called employer's portion. This is because the payroll tax paid by the employer is included in the total amount of money the employer has available to pay labour-related costs. In other words, payroll taxes reduce potential wage and salary payments. Since no corresponding reduction can be expected in the price of the products that the employee will want to purchase, the payroll tax, in effect, burdens the employee.

While both of these arguments have been framed in terms of employees and their wages and salaries, it is clear that taxes burden capital income as well. For example, a general sales tax reduces the purchasing power of all income, not just wage and salary income. As a result, it is appropriate to view the burden of the general sales tax as falling on all forms of earned income, including interest income and dividends. All of the estimates of tax burden constructed in this study, therefore, allocate the burden of general sales taxes in proportion to all earned income received by a family. In practical terms, this means that if general sales taxes amount to 5% of total Canadian income in a particular year, we add 5% of a family's total earned income to the family's tax bill when we calculate how much tax the family pays.

In computing this burden of general sales tax, income that a family receives from government is explicitly ignored. This is because the payments received from government such as Old Age Security and the Canada Pension Plan have been, and currently are, either directly or indirectly indexed to the general level of prices to offset the effects of inflation. As the general price level rises in step with the sales tax, the purchasing power of transfers from government is not permitted to fall. As a consequence, the general sales tax does not have the effect of burdening income in this form and it would be inappropriate to allocate any part of the burden of general sales taxes to this sort of income.

Excise taxes

While the burdens of a general sales tax and payroll taxes are relatively straightforward to assign, the assignment of particular excise taxes is more elusive. Whereas a general sales tax increases all prices and hence reduces the purchasing power of all incomes not derived from transfers from government, particular taxes on commodities usually affect only the price of that commodity. For example, excise taxes imposed on liquor, motor vehicles, and fuels affect only the prices of those products. Ultimately, of course, they may affect a whole range of prices—fuel taxes and motor-vehicle taxes affect the price of transportation. These taxes may, therefore, have an overall effect although levied only on a particular product.

In light of these considerations, it had been the usual practice when calculating tax burdens to allocate the burden of particular excise taxes according to the consumption of those items. Studies of the 1976 tax burden published by the Fraser Institute (Walker 1976; Pipes and Walker 1979) employed this methodology. Following this methodology, however, gives rise to a variety of problems. First, only the first-round effects of the excise tax are incorporated and, hence, the actual distribution of the tax burden may differ substantially from the estimate. Second, this method may not even provide good estimates of the first-round effects of the tax because the relative burden of a particular tax borne by a family is determined not by the family's consumption of the taxed item but by the fraction of the family's income spent on the item relative to the national average.

In view of these problems with the traditional approach, and given that the proportions of income spent on different items by various income groups do not vary widely from the average, we decided for the purposes of this study to distribute excise taxes in the same way as general sales taxes; that is to say, this study assumes that excise taxes burden total incomes—excluding government transfers to persons. So, the answer to the question, "Who pays the indirect taxes?" is ultimately a straightforward one. Although indirect taxes appear in a variety of forms, they burden the income that the family earns.

Other taxes by other names

In addition to "formal" taxes levied by government, there are a variety of other government policies that have the same effect as taxes but are not normally identified as such: the costs of complying with tax laws and regulations, the regulations that restrict our activities every day, price support for producers of agricultural products, and import duties and quotas to assist clothing and textile manufacturers. There is no difference in principle between this sort of tax and other hidden taxes. These "taxes" do not show up in records of government revenue and precise estimates of their size are difficult to make but we cannot ignore their existence.

Compliance and administrative costs of taxation

Compliance costs are those expenses incurred by individuals, families, and businesses to comply with tax regulations including the time and expenses incurred to maintain proper records, undertake tax planning, file necessary reports, and calculate required remittances. Administrative costs are those incurred by governments to collect taxes and enforce tax regulations.

Compliance costs of taxation in Canada were estimated at between $16.2 billion to $25.0 billion in 2005 while administrative costs were estimated at between $2.7 billion and $5.8 billion (Vaillancourt et al., 2007). In total, compliance and administrative costs in Canada ranged between $18.9 billion and $30.8 billion for 2005, representing between 1.4% and 2.3% of gross domestic product (GDP).

Regulatory taxation

In general, a government can achieve a given objective either by taxation and subsidization or by regulation. Rather than the current practice of imposing import quotas to help Canadian clothing manufacturers, the federal government could provide assistance by giving them a direct subsidy financed from general tax revenue. That the government uses regulation to convey the subsidy should not blind us to the fact that a subsidy is being provided and that it is the Canadian consumer who is paying for it.

For governments, regulation seems a painless way of advancing their public policy without spending tax dollars directly. The reality of regulation, however, is not so benign since it increases the cost of doing business. Governments bear little of the cost of regulation: their costs are limited to the administrative share while businesses and consumers must bear the much larger cost of complying with the regulations.

According to a 2001 study by the Fraser Institute, the compliance cost of all federal, provincial, and municipal regulations amounted to $103 billion in 1997/1998 (Jones and Graf, 2001). This works out to $13,700 per family of four. The federal and provincial governments legislated over 117,000 regulations over the 24-year period investigated in the study; the federal government alone passed an average of 1,042 regulations per year. "Regulation affects almost every aspect of our lives, including what we listen to on the radio, the prices and quality of the food we eat, the safety features in our cars, who is allowed to deliver our mail, where we are permitted to smoke and drink, and how we are restricted in the use of our property" (Jones and Graf 2001: 3).

Two recent reports have more narrowly estimated the cost of regulation for business. A 2005 survey by Statistics Canada of small and medium-sized businesses estimated average regulatory compliance costs of $2,839 per business. A survey by the Canadian Federation of Independent Business (CFIB) estimated the cost to Canadian businesses of complying with regulations at approximately $33 billion annually (Jones et al., 2005).

Marketing-board taxes

There are dozens of cartels controlling farm products in Canada. These cartels or marketing boards generally have the effect of suppressing competition in the production of the product subject to the cartel and, consequently, they cause the price of the product to be higher than it would otherwise have been. The amount by which the marketing board price exceeds the price that would prevail in its absence—that is, in the open market—is a tax on the consumer and marketing boards ought to be viewed as a device for transferring money from consumers to producers. The Organisation for Economic Co-operation and Development (OECD) estimates that the implicit tax in the form of support for the market prices of agricultural products paid by Canadian consumers was $4.2 billion in 2006. Total household spending on food in Canada is roughly $86.9 billion; marketing boards and other implicit agricultural taxes add about $348 (4.9%) to the cost of the average Canadian family's food bill.

Canada and the OECD countries adopted a set of principles for agricultural policy reform in 1987. The OECD notes that substantial progress has been made in reducing the level of government support for producers (OECD, 2007a): prices received by Canadian farmers as a result of government support were 13% higher than world prices in the period from 2004 to 2006, down from 40% in the period from 1986 to 1988. In addition, total support to agriculture has decreased from 1.8% of GDP in the period from 1986 to 1988 to 0.8% in the period from 2004 to 2006. However, the OECD also warns that, "the level of support has been trending upward in the most recent years" (OECD, 2007a: 92).

Due to trade liberalization and internal reforms, the level of agricultural support in OECD countries is lower than in 1987 and this means lower implicit taxes for Canadians. If the Canadian governments return to reducing the level of support to agriculture, consumers will experience a further reduction in implicit taxes caused by government support of market prices.

Clothing and textile taxes

In November 1976, the federal government imposed a quota on imported clothing and textiles. Its purpose was to limit the importation of inexpensive clothing and textiles and so protect Canadian clothing and textile manufacturers from competition. The associated decline in competition for the Canadian consumer's clothing-expenditure dollar undoubtedly produced a higher price for clothing than would otherwise have existed. The difference between the price for clothing that would have prevailed in the absence of the quota and the price that actually prevails is a tax on the consumer. Proceeds from this tax go directly to producers who are, in effect, being subsidized by the consumers.

Some of the burden associated with tariffs and quotas has been eliminated as a result of the North American Free Trade Agreement (NAFTA) among Canada, the United States, and Mexico. However, in many cases the principal source of cheaper products is not the United States but less developed countries. In value terms, 77.4% of textile imports into Canada come from developed countries while 71.5% of clothing imports come from developing countries (Canadian Textiles Institute, personal communication to Joel Emes, 1998).

The authors of *Free Trade between the United States and Canada* estimated that the total amount of tax levied in the form of tariff protection or other barriers to international competition was as high as 10.5% of Canada's Gross National Product (Wonnacott and Wonnacott, 1967: 299). Others have estimated the costs of tariffs at 8.2% of GDP in 1974 (Wonnacott, 1975) and 8.6% of GDP in 1976 (Harris and Cox, 1983). Canada has seen a significant reduction in tariff protection since these studies were completed. In 1981, import duties were equal to 3.6% of imports from other countries, by 1991 they were only 2.3%, and by 2006 they were down to 0.7%. However, a report by the World Trade Organization indicates concerns about market access for developing countries in certain areas: "... significant trade barriers still protect certain agricultural activities and foreign investment restrictions remain in areas such as telecommunications, audiovisual, and air and maritime transport" (World Trade Organization, 2007). Additional reforms in these areas will reduce the hidden taxes imposed on Canadians.

Deferred taxation

During his budget statement in November 1978, the Honourable Jean Chrétien, then federal Minister of Finance, made much of the fact that, because the personal income-tax structure had been indexed to inflation, there had, in effect, been a reduction in personal income taxation compared to what would have prevailed in the absence of indexing. That is to say, exemptions had been increased by the rate of inflation and tax brackets had been shifted to ensure that incomes swollen by inflation would not be taxed more heavily on that account alone. While this change in the tax structure was indeed welcome, it did not represent a move towards a permanent reduction in the government's propensity to tax. The "reduction" in personal income-tax revenues, in fact, was accompanied—starting in 1975—by deficits in the federal government's accounts that were unprecedented in peacetime. Although this situation is not entirely attributable to the relative decline in personal income-tax revenues, it is clear that continued growth in income taxation would have meant a smaller deficit and a reduction in net cash requirements to be financed by issuing debt.

Accordingly, it has been standard practice in assessing the level of taxation in Canada to take into account the extent to which tax collections are merely deferred by current tax "reductions." In other words, in addition to calculating the total tax burden of all government operations in a given year, we have in the past calculated the balanced-budget tax burden, which included not only taxes levied now but also taxes that must be levied in the future to discharge debts acquired by the government to finance the current deficit. In recent years, there has been a dramatic shift away from deficit financing, or deferred taxation, in favour of balanced or surplus budgets. This shift has made the continued calculation of a balanced-budget tax burden unnecessary.

How much tax should Canadians pay?

In 1917, when he first introduced the Personal Income Tax, the Finance Minister, Sir Thomas White, was of the opinion that no Canadian should pay tax on income less than $2,000 if he were single and had no dependents. Married taxpayers, he said, should pay tax on income in excess of $3,000. The tax structure that ultimately evolved provided that single Canadians paid income tax on income in excess of $1,500, while married Canadians were exempted from the tax until their incomes exceeded $3,000. However, the very next year, this was reduced to $2,000 for a married taxpayer and $1,000 for single Canadians (Government of Canada, 1917).

While the tax structure has gone through many changes in the intervening years, it is interesting to ask how Canadians would be taxed if this initial view of the "ability to pay" had kept pace with developments in people's incomes. To answer this question we have adjusted the original exemption levels by the increase in inflation over the period since 1917. This adjustment yields an exemption level for 2007 of $21,161 for single taxpayers and $42,323 for married taxpayers. But actual personal credits for single and married taxpayers amounted to $9,600 and $19,200 in 2007, significantly less than the level of income that would have been exempt if the 1917 standard had continued in force. The reason for the disparity is that, over the years from 1917 to 1974, exemption levels were not indexed to the cost of living or the increase in family incomes; in fact, in a few years during the Depression, exemption levels were actually reduced. In addition, exemption levels and tax brackets were only partially indexed to inflation between 1986 and 1999.

Chapter 2
Personal Income Taxation in Canada

Personal income tax is the largest single source of government revenue. It follows, therefore, that the largest single tax paid by the average Canadian family is the income tax. This tax came into existence in 1917 as a "temporary" emergency measure to help finance the increasing debt incurred during World War I. Nothing, it seems, endures like the temporary.

The current income tax structure

Several significant changes to personal income taxation were announced or confirmed in 1999 and 2000. These changes include the re-indexation of exemptions and brackets and the move by the provinces from "tax-on-tax" assessment of personal income to "tax-on-income" assessment.

Bracket creep

Many Canadian taxpayers have been pushed into higher tax brackets and have seen the value of their basic exemption eroded in recent years because governments have not always adjusted brackets and exemptions to mitigate the effects of inflation. The best way to illustrate this problem, which is often called "bracket creep," is with an example. If a worker earning $29,000 in 2000 received a 5% raise to compensate for a 5% increase in prices, her income would increase to $30,450. This 5% raise would almost allow her to maintain her standard of living but falls short because she would now pay more income tax relative to her income than when she earned $29,000. Whereas all of the $29,000 was taxed at the 17% federal rate, the part of

$30,450 in excess of $29,000 is taxed at the 25% federal rate. In the 2000 budget, the federal government announced that it would index all brackets and exemptions to the inflation rate for the 2001 and subsequent taxation years, thus ending bracket creep in the federal personal income-tax system.

Tax-on-tax assessment and tax-on-income assessment

The federal and provincial governments share personal income taxation. Prior to 2000, most provinces based their personal income tax on the "basic federal tax." Residents of provinces other than Quebec determined their basic tax owing by multiplying the basic federal tax by the provincial tax rate; hence the term "tax-on-tax" applied to most of the provincial personal income-tax systems. Quebec has operated its own personal income-tax system since 1954 on the "tax-on-income" basis. Tax-on-income assessment parallels the federal personal income-tax calculation, with taxable income as the starting point for the tax calculation. British Columbia, Manitoba, New Brunswick, Nova Scotia, and Ontario introduced tax-on-income systems in 2000. Alberta, Saskatchewan, Prince Edward Island, Newfoundland and Labrador, and the territories introduced tax-on-income systems for 2001. Tax-on-income assessment gives the provincial governments more flexibility in changing their personal income-tax systems to suit the needs and priorities of their constituents. The switch to tax-on-income also protects provincial revenues from decreases in federal personal income tax that, in a tax-on-tax system, automatically translate into decreases in provincial personal income tax because they decrease the basic federal tax and, therefore, the base for the provincial tax calculation. For a good overview of these changes to the provincial personal income tax systems, see Ort and Perry (2000) and Treff and Perry (1999).

Combined income-tax rates

Table 2.1 presents the actual income-tax rates (combined federal and provincial) encountered by the average single individual at various levels of taxable income in 1990 through 2007. As the figures show, the minimum rate of tax in 2007 is 22.2%, payable on the range of taxable income from $1.00 to $37,178. The second rate is 32.56%, payable on the range of taxable income from $37,179 to $74,357. The third rate is 38.48%, payable on the range of taxable income from $74,358 to $120,887. The maximum rate of 42.92% is payable on taxable income in excess of $120,887.[1] These rates are

1 ◆ For 2007, a nominal provincial rate of 48% has been used. This represents the federal rate levied on income earned out of any province.

the marginal rates of tax encountered as one moves from one level of taxable income to the next. Table 2.2 shows the combined federal and provincial marginal tax rates for a single individual in each province at three levels of income. An equally interesting series of calculations shows the amount of tax an individual pays on a given amount of total, rather than taxable, income (see table 2.3).

Table 2.1: Combined federal & provincial personal income-tax rates, 1990–2007

1990 Taxable income	1990 Rate (%)	1995 Taxable income	1995 Rate (%)	2000 Taxable income	2000 Rate (%)	2007 Taxable income	2007 Rate (%)
$1–$28,275	26.61	*$1–$29,590*	26.35	*$1–$30,004*	25.16	*$1–$37,178*	22.20
$28,276–$56,550	40.69	*$29,591–$59,180*	40.30	*$30,005–$60,009*	37.00	*$37,179–$74,357*	32.56
$56,551–$69,965	45.39	*$59,181–$62,192*	44.95	*$60,010–$74,240*	42.92	*$74,358–$120,887*	38.48
$69,966 & above	46.84	*$62,193 & above*	46.40	*$74,241 & above*	44.37	*$120,888 & above*	42.92

Sources: Canadian Tax Foundation, *The National Finances* 1990 and 1991; *Finances of the Nation* 1995, 2000, & 2007; 2007 federal and provincial budgets; calculations by the authors.

Table 2.2: Personal income tax for a single taxpayer, combined federal and provincial marginal rates (%), 2007

	Income $20,000	Income $50,000	Income $100,000
Newfoundland & Labrador	23.0	37.0	44.0
Prince Edward Island	23.1	35.8	44.4
Nova Scotia	27.2	37.0	44.3
New Brunswick	28.8	38.1	43.1
Quebec	27.7	38.4	45.7
Ontario	25.6	31.2	43.4
Manitoba	25.2	35.0	43.4
Saskatchewan	24.3	35.0	39.0
Alberta	23.3	32.0	36.0
British Columbia	22.2	30.2	40.7

Sources: Canadian Tax Foundation, *Finances of the Nation 2007.*

Table 2.3: Combined federal and provincial personal income tax and tax rate (single taxpayer with no dependants), 2007

Total income ($)	Total tax payable ($)	Rate (%)	Total income ($)	Total tax payable ($)	Rate (%)
7,500	0	0.0	25,000	3,197	12.8
10,000	0	0.0	30,000	4,307	14.4
12,500	422	3.4	50,000	10,076	20.2
15,000	977	6.5	100,000	27,873	27.9
17,500	1,532	8.8	200,000	69,866	34.9
20,000	2,087	10.4			

Sources: Provincial budgets; Canada Revenue Agency, tax forms; calculations by the authors.

Income-tax rates for couples and families

The situation can be slightly different for families because there are credits permitted for the dependent spouse. Support of children also eases somewhat the tax burden on the taxpayer. In perusing tax rates for the average family of four presented in table 2.4, the reader should bear in mind that this schedule of rates is not applicable to all families. In many cases, both adult members of the family declare taxable income and, since each files a separate return, tax rates for individuals apply. Of course, this is to the advantage of the taxpayers. If, for example, a childless couple who are both working have

Table 2.4: Combined federal & provincial personal income tax, Canada Child Tax Benefit, and tax rate (married taxpayer with two dependant children under 16 years of age), 2007

Total income ($)	Total tax payable ($)	Canada Child Tax Benefit ($)	Net tax ($)	Rate (%)
15,000	0	6,244	(6,244)	(41.6)
17,500	0	6,244	(6,244)	(35.7)
20,000	0	6,244	(6,244)	(31.2)
25,000	1,066	5,492	(4,426)	(17.7)
30,000	2,176	4,599	(2,424)	(8.1)
50,000	7,944	2,327	5,617	11.2
100,000	25,742	1,039	24,703	24.7
200,000	67,735	0	67,735	33.9

Sources: Provincial budgets; Canada Revenue Agency, tax forms; calculations by the authors.

the same income—say $25,000 per year—they pay total tax of about $6,394 when they file as individuals. If the family's total income of $50,000 were earned by only one of them, the total tax payable would be about $7,944—a difference of $1,550. In other words, if the family's income is earned by one family member, the family pays a gross tax rate of 15.9% but, if this income is composed of two salaries, the tax rate is only 12.8%. The difference between the two tax rates rises as family income increases until very high income levels are reached (see table 2.5). This difference between the tax rates of families with a single income and those with double incomes affects many of the other calculations in the remainder of this book. In particular, income-tax payments shown in the various composite tax tables in chapter 3 reflect the fact that, on average, tax payments are made by a mixture of single-taxpayer and double-taxpayer families.

Table 2.5: Tax rates for a married couple, 2007

Total family income ($)	One income earner		Two income earners	
	Tax ($)	Tax rate (%)	Tax ($)	Tax rate (%)
15,000	0	0.0	0	0.0
20,000	0	0.0	0	0.0
25,000	1,066	4.3	844	3.4
30,000	2,176	7.3	1,954	6.5
50,000	7,944	15.9	6,394	12.8
100,000	25,742	25.7	20,152	20.2
200,000	67,735	33.9	55,746	27.9

Sources: Provincial budgets; Canada Revenue Agency, tax forms; calculations by the authors.

Who pays income taxes?

According to data for 2005 from the Canada Revenue Agency (formerly Revenue Canada), a total of $134.4 billion in income taxes was paid by individuals and, as table 2.6 shows, 24.9% was paid by individuals with incomes below $50,000. Individuals with incomes below $60,000 paid 43.3% of the total income tax bill. In fact, 23.2% of all income taxes were paid by individuals with yearly incomes in the relatively narrow range of $20,000 to $50,000.

As column 5 of table 2.6 shows, nearly one-half of returns were filed by individuals with incomes of less than $20,000. This proportion reflects the large number of part-time workers, students employed during the summer,

Table 2.6: Income, taxes, and tax returns by income group, 2005 tax year

Total income assessed ($)	Total tax paid by …	
	this income group (%)	all groups at or below this income group (%)
loss or nil	0.0	0.0
$1 – $10,000	0.1	0.1
$10,000 – $15,000	0.5	0.5
$15,000 – $20,000	1.3	1.8
$20,000 – $25,000	2.1	3.9
$25,000 – $30,000	3.1	7.0
$30,000 – $35,000	3.9	10.9
$35,000 – $40,000	4.4	15.3
$40,000 – $45,000	4.8	20.0
$45,000 – $50,000	4.9	24.9
$50,000 – $60,000	9.5	34.5
$60,000 – $70,000	8.8	43.3
$70,000 – $80,000	7.6	50.9
$80,000 – $90,000	5.9	56.8
$90,000 – $100,000	4.5	61.3
$100,000 – $150,000	11.8	73.1
$150,000 – $250,000	8.1	81.2
$250,000 +	18.8	100.0

Sources: Canada Revenue Agency, *Income Statistics 2007—2005 Tax Year*; calculations by authors.

and other intermittent workers earning low incomes. These taxpayers generated only 1.8% of total tax revenue, while the top one-third of taxpayers—those declaring income of $35,000 or more—contributed 89.1% of the total income-tax bill.

An interesting aspect of the information in table 2.6 is the relation between taxes paid and income declared. For example, while 10.9% of the total income-tax bill was paid by individuals with incomes below $35,000, column 6 reveals that this group earned 27.3% of all the income declared. So, those earning incomes below $35,000 paid a smaller proportion of the total tax bill than their share of total earned income might suggest. On the other hand, the top 33.0% of taxpayers, those who had incomes in excess of $35,000, paid about 89.1% of the total tax bill, while receiving only 72.7% of total income earned.

Total returns filed by ...		Total income declared by ...	
this income group (%)	all groups at or below this income group (%)	this income group (%)	all groups at or below this income group (%)
1.3	1.3	(0.1)	(0.1)
20.2	21.5	2.7	2.6
11.8	33.3	4.1	6.8
10.0	43.3	4.8	11.6
7.5	50.8	4.7	16.3
6.8	57.6	5.2	21.5
6.4	64.0	5.8	27.3
5.7	69.7	5.9	33.3
4.9	74.6	5.8	39.1
4.1	78.7	5.4	44.5
6.3	85.0	9.6	54.1
4.5	89.5	8.2	62.2
3.1	92.6	6.6	68.8
2.0	94.6	4.8	73.6
1.3	95.9	3.5	77.0
2.5	98.5	8.3	85.4
1.0	99.4	5.0	90.3
0.6	100.0	9.7	100.0

The reason for this, of course, is that the income-tax structure is "progressive." That is, it takes a larger fraction from high incomes than it does from low incomes, as is clear from the tax rates presented in table 2.4. Sales taxes also contribute to progressivity, even though everyone pays the same rate irrespective of income, because sales-tax rebates vary inversely with income. Furthermore, many income transfers from the state are indexed to the price of goods so that, as the price rises due to a sales tax, so do the transfers. This eases the burden of sales taxes to the poor.

Chapter 3
How Much Tax Do You Really Pay?

WHILE INCOME TAX IS the single largest tax category, it represents less than half of the total taxes paid by the average Canadian family. This chapter expands the discussion to include all taxes that Canadians pay.

How much income do you really earn?

Cash income

In order to calculate properly how much tax a person or group pays, it is necessary first to determine income. This is a complex calculation because there are a multitude of sources of income other than wages and salaries. This chapter explains the method for deriving the income figures used in subsequent sections.

The ultimate goal of income calculations is to determine the total income a Canadian citizen would have if there were no taxes of any sort and other factors remained unchanged. To arrive at such a figure, it is necessary to determine all the sources of income a person might have and all of the taxes that would have been paid on this income before the person received it. The first layer of sources is easily discovered: wages, salaries, interest from savings bonds, or rent from the in-law suite in the basement are the sorts of items that make up cash income.

Cash income and under-reporting

In its regular surveys of household income, Statistics Canada finds that people typically omit some income items when they estimate their cash income.

That is, they under-report their income. The particular items omitted vary from family to family but, on average, families tend to underestimate their total income by 4% to 12%. Items that might be omitted include miscellaneous interest income, income from "moonlighting," and so on. Fortunately, Statistics Canada does have a comprehensive measure of income in the National Accounts framework, upon which estimates of cash income used in this study are based.

It may be useful at this stage to provide an example based on a fictitious family. In order to make the example as comprehensive as possible, it is assumed that the family has income from all of the sources identified in the study—an unlikely circumstance for any real family. The example is presented in table 3.1.

Table 3.1: Cash income, 2007

Wages & salaries	$46,881
Income from farm operations	$36
Unincorporated non-farm income	$2,697
Interest	$1,710
Dividends	$661
Private and government pension payments	$4,043
Old age pension payments	$2,125
Other transfers from government	$8,344
Cash income	$66,496

Source: The Fraser Institute's Canadian Tax Simulator 2007.

Total income

In addition to cash income, most families also have various forms of non-cash income that must be included in a comprehensive income figure. For example, most wage and salary earners receive fringe benefits as a condition of their employment and their income also includes the investment income accumulated by their pension plan and the interest accumulated—though not paid—on their insurance policies.

At a higher level of subtlety, a comprehensive income total should also include a number of other income sources. For example, income must be imputed on account of interest-free loans that people make. The interest foregone is, in fact, implicit income in the form of a gift.

Profits not paid out as dividends by corporations but held in the form of retained earnings are income of the shareholders of the corporation, even though they do not receive it in the year in which it is reported. Finally, food consumed by farm operators is evaluated at market price and attributed to farm operators as income.

Again, to make the calculation clear, the accumulated total income is shown in table 3.2 for a fictitious family that is assumed to have income from all sources.

Table 3.2: Total income, 2007

Cash income	$66,496
Fringe benefits from employment	$9,873
Investment income from insurance companies	$804
Investment income from pension plans	$2,534
Imputed interest	$351
Value of food from farms	$11
Corporate retained earnings	$4,035
Total income	$84,104

Source: The Fraser Institute's Canadian Tax Simulator 2007.

Total income before tax

Some of the income earned by Canadians is taxed before they receive it. For example, shareholders receive dividends on corporate profits after corporate profit taxes have been paid. In the absence of taxes, the dividends or retained earnings of the shareholder would have been higher. Therefore, in order to arrive at total income before tax, it is necessary to add the tax on corporate profits collected from corporations. Similarly, if there were no property taxes, net after-tax rental income would be higher than it actually is. Therefore, before-tax income must be augmented by the amount of property taxes paid.

Indirect and hidden taxes reduce the effective income available to Canadians because they increase the prices of items that people buy with their incomes. In effect, income after tax is less, in terms of what it will buy, than it was before the tax. In order to arrive at an estimate of income before tax it is necessary to add to incomes the reduction brought about by indirect taxes. Payroll taxes levied on firms are, as noted earlier, effectively paid by employees, because the taxes reduce the amount of money available to pay wages and salaries. Accordingly, it is necessary to add the amount of payroll taxes to employees' incomes to arrive at an estimate of total income before tax.

Table 3.3 presents an example of a complete income calculation for a fictitious family that is assumed to have income from all of the income sources identified in the study and to have paid all of the identified taxes.

Table 3.3: Total income before tax, 2007

Wages & salaries	$46,881
Income from farm operations	$36
Unincorporated non-farm income	$2,697
Interest	$1,710
Dividends	$661
Private and government pension payments	$4,043
Old age pension payments	$2,125
Other transfers from government	$8,344
Cash income	$66,496
Plus	
Fringe benefits from employment	$9,873
Investment income from insurance companies	$804
Investment income from pension plans	$2,534
Imputed interest	$351
Value of food from farms	$11
Corporate retained earnings	$4,035
Total income	$84,104
Plus	
Property taxes	$2,682
Profit taxes	$3,300
Indirect taxes	$13,436
Total income before tax	$103,522

Source: The Fraser Institute's Canadian Tax Simulator 2007.

Calculating the total tax bill

The tax calculation for the average Canadian family consists of adding up the various taxes that the family pays. Hidden taxes, such as taxes on tobacco and alcohol, are allocated according to the method described in chapter 1. To preserve consistency, the family used for the example of the tax calculation in table 3.4 is the same family used in the income calculation.

A note on the calculation of Tax Freedom Day

The calculations in this chapter underlie our calculation of Tax Freedom Day, the day of the year when the average family has earned enough income to pay the total tax bill imposed on it by all levels of government. We are occasionally asked why we calculate Tax Freedom Day using cash income rather than total income before tax. We use cash income because the main purpose of Tax Freedom Day is to convey the size of the total tax bill imposed on

Table 3.4: Tax bill of the average Canadian family, 2007

Total cash income	$66,496
Total income before tax	$103,522
Taxes	
Income taxes	$9,816
Sales taxes	$4,495
Liquor, tobacco, amusement & other excise taxes	$1,764
Auto , fuel & motor vehicle licence taxes	$722
Social security, medical & hospital taxes	$5,999
Property taxes	$2,682
Import duties	$240
Profits tax	$3,300
Natural resource taxes	$539
Other taxes	$655
Total taxes	$30,213
Taxes as a percentage of total cash income	45.4%
Taxes as a percentage of total income before tax	29.2%

Source: The Fraser Institute's Canadian Tax Simulator 2007.

Canadian families in a format that is easily understood. If we told people that taxes are 30% of their total income before tax, they would have a large task ahead of them to estimate all the types of income that must be included to arrive at this measure of income. Many people think of cash income (wages and salaries, government transfers, pension payments, interest and dividends, farm income, and self-employment income) as their total income. Most do not consider all the other types of income they earn but do not see (including corporate retained earnings, the investment income on their pension plans, and indirect taxes) as part of their total income. For example, if we were to report that the total tax burden for the average family was 30% most people with a family cash income of $66,000 would estimate their tax bill at $19,800 when it is actually closer to $30,000. The crucial piece of information is that governments extracted $30,000 from your family; the particular definition of income is secondary. Cash income is a useful tool in describing the tax burden because it does not force people to go through arithmetical gymnastics to arrive at their total income before tax to get an idea of how large the total tax burden is. Canadians can calculate their personal Tax Freedom Day using the Fraser Institute's *Personal Tax Freedom Day Calculator* at <www.fraserinstitute.org>.

Chapter 4
The Canadian Consumer Tax Index and Tax Freedom Day

IT IS ALWAYS SATISFYING TO FIND ONE NUMBER, or index, that neatly summarizes a complicated issue. It is seldom the case that such a number exists. IQ scores, for instance, do not say everything about an individual's intelligence and the speed of a computer chip can only give a rough idea of how that computer will perform. The same is true of Canadian taxes. Our system is complex and there is no single number that can give us a complete idea of who pays how much, and how the system has changed over time. That said, we can introduce two of the better indicators of the state of the tax burden of the average Canadian family: the Canadian Consumer Tax Index and Tax Freedom Day.

The Canadian Consumer Tax Index

For individual taxpayers, the most interesting variable is how much tax they actually have to pay. In the Fraser Institute's first tax study, *How Much Tax Do You Really Pay?* (Walker, 1976b), we devised an index that we called the Canadian Consumer Tax Index (CCTI). Its purpose was to provide a summary that would tell at a glance what has been happening to the tax bill faced by the average Canadian family over the years since 1961.

Some readers of that book found the tax index too simple: it failed to take into account how the tax money was spent by governments and, therefore, showed only one side of the ledger (McGillivray, 1976). In our analyses, revenue collection and government spending are considered separately because they are distinct government actions. Government spending is considered in various publications including *Government Spending Facts 2* (Horry and Walker 1994), and our government report cards (Law, Markowitz, and Mihlar, 1997; Boucher, 1998; Chera and Mihlar, 1998; Clemens and Emes, 2001; Clemens et al., 2003). Further, the index in that first study and in all subsequent studies has been widely used by financial and consumer affairs columnists across the country to describe how the Canadian tax system has evolved. Moreover, it has been in continuous use ever since its release and has been described as the most up-to-date measure of the extent of Canadian taxation.

What is the Canadian Consumer Tax Index?

The Canadian Consumer Tax Index tracks the total tax bill paid by a Canadian family with average income. The "consumer" in question is the taxpaying family, which can be thought of as consuming government services. The Consumer Price Index measures the average price that consumers pay for the goods and services that they buy of their own choice. The CCTI measures the price of goods and services that government buys on behalf of its constituents (see table 4.1 and figure 4.1).

The CCTI is constructed by calculating the difference in the tax bill of an average Canadian family from the tax bill in the base year of 1961 for each of the years included in the index. Now, while each of these families had average income in the year selected, the family is not the same one from year to year. The objective is not to trace the tax experience of a particular family but rather to plot the experience of a family that was average in each year.

Table 4.1: The Canadian Consumer Tax Index (1961 = 100)

1961	100	1990	1,116	2002	1,549
1969	186	1992	1,047	2004	1,617
1974	324	1994	1,097	2006	1,771
1976	357	1996	1,192	2007	1,804
1981	682	1998	1,290		
1985	886	2000	1,480		

Source: The Fraser Institute's Canadian Tax Simulator 2007.

Figure 4.1: The Canadian Consumer Tax Index, 1961–2007

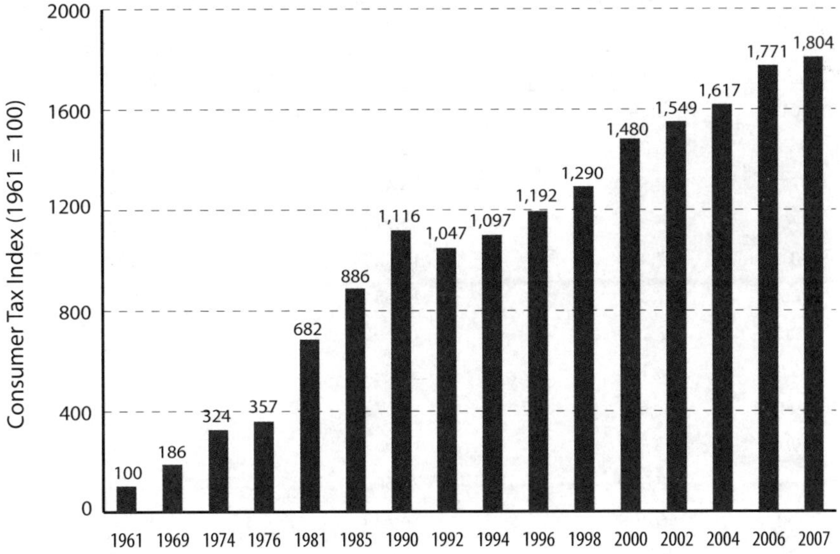

Source: Table 4.1.

The CCTI thus answers the following question: How has the tax burden of the average family changed since 1961, bearing in mind that the average family has itself changed in that period? We can note, for example, that the average family in 2006 is headed by an older person, one who is more likely to own a car and a house, and has fewer members than the average family in 1961 (Dominion Bureau of Statistics, 1962; Statistics Canada, 1983, 2006a). Most important, the family's earned income increased by 1,230% between 1961 and 2007.

The basis of the CCTI is the total tax calculation presented in the "Tax Bill" column of table 4.2. Calculations of income and tax were made for a selection of years beginning in 1961 and ending in 2007. The results show that the tax bill of the average Canadian family has increased by 1,704% from 1961 and that the index has a value of 1,804 for 2007 (see table 4.5).

Part of that increase reflects the effects of inflation. In order to eliminate the portion of the increase due to the erosion of purchasing power, we have also calculated the tax index in real dollars—that is, dollars of 2007 purchasing power. While this adjustment has the effect of reducing the steepness of the index's path over time, the real-dollar tax index, nevertheless, increased by 154.1% over the period (see table 4.3).

Table 4.2: Taxes paid by the average Canadian family (families and unattached individuals), 1961–2007

	Average cash income ($)	Tax bill ($)	Increase in tax bill over base year (%)
1961	5,000	1,675	—
1969	8,000	3,117	86
1974	12,500	5,429	224
1976	16,500	5,979	257
1981	27,980	11,429	582
1985	32,309	14,834	786
1990	43,170	18,693	1,016
1992	43,178	17,545	947
1994	43,651	18,370	997
1996	45,047	19,964	1,092
1998	48,039	21,603	1,190
2000	53,469	24,789	1,380
2002	56,642	25,953	1,449
2004	58,909	27,077	1,517
2006	64,273	29,672	1,671
2007	66,496	30,213	1,704

Source: The Fraser Institute's Canadian Tax Simulator 2007.

Table 4.3: Inflation-adjusted tax bill and Consumer Tax Index, 1961–2007

	Tax Bill (2007 $)	Percentage change in taxes since 1961		Tax Bill (2007 $)	Percentage change in taxes since 1961
1961	11,890	—	1994	23,890	100.9
1969	17,634	48.3	1996	25,028	110.5
1974	23,094	94.2	1998	26,371	121.8
1976	21,426	80.2	2000	28,959	143.6
1981	25,733	116.4	2002	28,925	143.3
1985	26,242	120.7	2004	28,823	142.4
1990	26,573	123.5	2006	30,307	154.9
1992	23,278	95.8	2007	30,213	154.1

Sources: The Fraser Institute's Canadian Tax Simulator 2007; Statistics Canada, *The Consumer Price Index*, catalogue 62-001-XPB.

What the Canadian Consumer Tax Index shows

The dramatic increase in the tax burden of the average family over the period from 1961 to 2007 was produced by the interaction of a number of factors. First, there was a dramatic increase in incomes over the period that has generated a substantial increase in the family's tax bill. Indeed, average cash income has grown 1,230% since 1961. The second contributing factor was an increase in the tax rate faced by the average family from 33.5% in 1961 to 45.4% in 2007.

What if we got rid of the debt?

A deficit is the amount that government must borrow in any given year to finance spending in excess of revenue. Over the years, these deficits accumulate. This accumulation is known as the debt. All debt must one day be paid off, either by increased taxes or reduced services. There is simply no getting around this fact. Getting rid of deficits is not the same as getting rid of the debt. How would the average Canadian family's tax burden change if all levels of government decided to eliminate their debts by the year 2027? Assuming a favourable growth rate for real income of 4%, population growth of 0.8%, and no change in government spending per capita, the average Canadian family's tax bill would rise by $3,511 in the first year to pay off the debt within 20 years. The average family's tax rate would jump from 45.4% in 2007 to 50.7% in 2008 and gradually fall to 27.1% in 2027 as seen in figure 4.2.

Figure 4.2: The impact of gross government debt repayment on the average Canadian family, 2007–2027

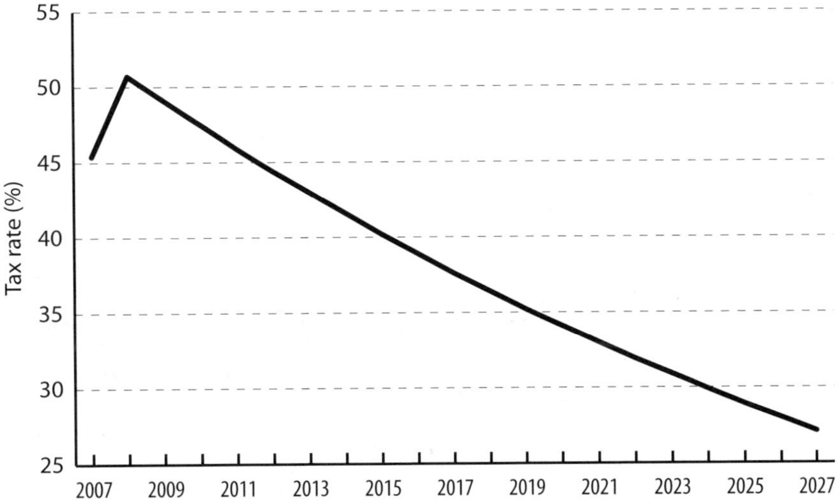

Sources: Statistics Canada, Financial Management System, 2007; calculations by authors.

Taxes compared to the necessities of life

To gauge the significance of the increase in the tax bill faced by Canadian families it is necessary to compare its evolution to other major expenditures of the average family. Table 4.4 and figure 4.3 compare the average dollar amount of family cash income and total taxes paid with family expenditures on shelter, food, and clothing. It is clear that taxation has become the most significant item that consumers face in their budgets and taxes have grown more rapidly than any other single item.

In 1961, the average family had to use 56.5% of its cash income to provide itself with shelter, food, and clothing. In the same year, 33.5% of the

Table 4.4: Income, taxes, and selected expenditures of the average Canadian family (dollars)

	Average cash income	Average tax bill	Average expenditures[1]		
			Shelter[2]	Food	Clothing
1961	5,000	1,675	1,130	1,259	435
1969	8,000	3,117	1,497	1,634	654
1974	12,500	5,429	2,294	2,320	886
1976	16,500	5,979	3,134	2,838	1,119
1981	27,980	11,429	5,381	4,440	1,499
1985	32,309	14,834	6,984	4,899	2,141
1990	43,170	18,693	8,776	5,745	2,234
1992	43,178	17,545	9,607	6,024	2,215
1994	43,651	18,370	9,592	6,066	2,116
1996	45,047	19,964	9,577	6,108	2,017
1998	48,039	21,603	10,159	6,016	2,123
2000	53,469	24,789	10,590	6,350	2,216
2002	56,642	25,953	11,566	6,905	2,330
2004	58,909	27,077	12,110	7,127	2,350
2006	64,273	29,672	12,716	7,424	2,418
2007	66,496	30,213	13,144	7,622	2,416

Note 1: All expenditure items include indirect taxes.
Note 2: Average Shelter Expenditures for years prior to 1998 are estimates. The estimate is to take account of a change in the definition of shelter between the Family Expenditure Survey and the Survey of Household Expenditures.
Sources: Statistics Canada, *Urban Family Expenditure*, cat. 62-549, 62-547, 62-544, 62-537, 62-535, 62-541, 62-525, 62-555; 1990, 1992, and 1996 Family Expenditure Surveys, cat. 62-555; 1998, 2001, 2004, 2005 Survey of Household Spending; The Consumer Price Index, 62-001-XPB; The Fraser Institute's Canadian Tax Simulator 2007.

Figure 4.3: Taxes and basic expenditures of the average Canadian family, 1961–2007

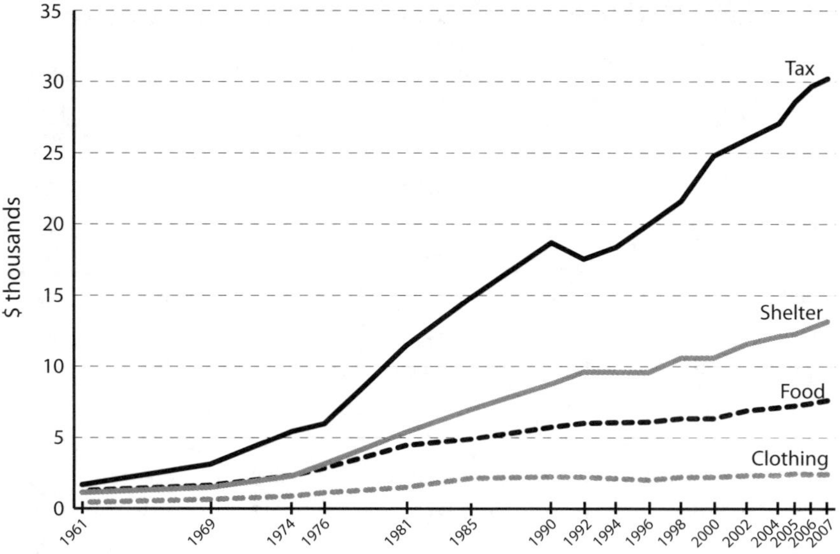

Notes: Data for some years have been interpolated; all years shown have full data. All expenditure items include indirect taxes. *Nota bene* that measurement of shelter has changed; see note on Table 4.4 for more information.
Source: Table 4.4.

family's income went to governments as tax. By 1981, the situation had been reversed and 40.8% of the income was taken by the governments in the form of taxes, while 40.5% was used to provide the family with shelter, food, and clothing. In 2007, the proportion of income consumed by taxes the average family spent 34.9% of its income on the necessities of life while 45.4% of its cash income went to taxes.

Table 4.5 and figure 4.4 shows the Canadian Consumer Tax Index relative to income and other expenditure indices. Average cash income rose by 1,230% between 1961 and 2007, prices rose by 610%, expenditures on shelter by 1,063%, food by 505%, and clothing by 455%. Meanwhile, the tax bill of the average family grew by 1,704%.

Tax Freedom Day

The Canadian Consumer Tax Index is only one tool for evaluating the Canadian tax system. Another easily understood and revealing measure is the Tax Freedom Day of the average Canadian family. For the purposes of calculating Tax Freedom Day, the average Canadian family is the family

Table 4.5: Income, tax, and expenditure indices (1961 = 100)

	Average cash income	Canadian Consumer Tax Index	Average Consumer Price Index	Average expenditures[1]		
				Shelter	Food	Clothing
1961	100	100	100	100	100	100
1969	160	186	125	132	130	150
1974	250	324	167	203	184	204
1976	330	357	198	277	225	257
1981	560	682	315	476	353	345
1985	646	886	401	618	389	492
1990	863	1,116	499	776	456	514
1992	864	1,047	535	850	478	509
1994	873	1,097	546	849	482	486
1996	901	1,192	566	847	485	464
1998	961	1,290	582	899	478	488
2000	1,069	1,480	608	937	504	509
2002	1,133	1,549	637	1,023	548	536
2004	1,178	1,617	667	1,071	566	540
2006	1,285	1,771	695	1,125	590	556
2007	1,330	1,804	710	1,163	605	555
	Percentage increase from 1961 to 2007					
	1,230	1,704	610	1,063	505	455

General note: All figures in this table are converted to indices by dividing each series in table 4.4 by its value in 1961, and then multiplying that figure by 100.
Note 1: All expenditure items include indirect taxes.
Source: Table 4.4; The Fraser Institute's Canadian Tax Simulator 2007.

whose income is the average income of all families with two or more members. Tax Freedom Day is that day of the year when the average family has done enough work to pay the total tax bill imposed on it by the federal, provincial, and municipal governments. It is calculated as the percentage of cash income the family pays in tax multiplied by 365 days to arrive at the number of days of work required to pay the total tax bill. If 50% of one's income goes to taxes, then one must work one half the year for government, and one's Tax Freedom Day falls on July 2. In 1961, Tax Freedom Day fell on May 3. Since then, it has advanced 48 days, so that in 2007 it fell on June 20. Canadians can calculate their personal Tax Freedom Day using the Fraser Institute's *Personal Tax Freedom Day Calculator* at <www.fraserinstitute.org>.

Figure 4.4: How the Canadian Consumer Tax Index has increased relative to other indices, 1961–2007

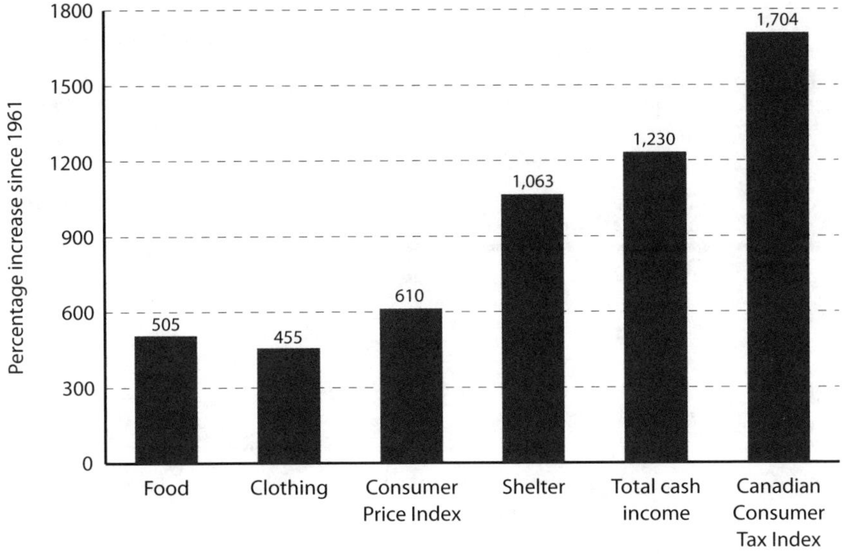

Source: Table 4.5.

Chapter 5
The Relative Tax Burden

How much do I pay? This is the first question that people ask about the tax system. Tax Freedom Day and the Canadian Consumer Tax Index discussed in the last chapter give a rough answer to this query. The next thing people want to know is how much are others paying? Are some paying less than others? These are more complicated questions because they call for a broad view of what the tax system does. Some in the media and many social-activist groups believe these questions have a clear and simple answer: the "rich" pay no taxes and the poor are getting "shafted by the system." In this chapter, we suggest that the answers are not so simple. We look at all income groups and how their relative income and tax positions have changed between 1961 and 2007. A reasonable analysis of these numbers points to a different conclusion than that presented by groups that claim Canada's tax system needs to be more progressive than it is.

The distribution of income

In order to analyze the relative income and tax positions of Canadians, we have divided all Canadian families into three, broad income groups based on income deciles. The first income decile is one of 10 groups that result from arranging families according to their total income before tax, from lowest to highest, and then selecting the 10% of families with the lowest incomes; the second decile is the next 10% of families, and so on. The lowest income group includes the families in the bottom three deciles; the middle group includes the next four deciles; the upper group includes the top three deciles. The resulting groups are presented in table 5.1 and illustrated in figure 5.1.

Table 5.1: Decile distribution (%) of income before tax

	Income Groups		
	Lower 3 deciles (%)	Middle 4 deciles (%)	Upper 3 deciles (%)
1961	10.8	35.6	53.6
1972	9.0	33.1	57.9
1976	8.8	31.7	59.5
1981	10.0	34.9	55.0
1985	10.2	35.1	54.7
1990	8.7	33.9	57.4
1992	7.6	30.6	61.7
1994	7.9	30.7	61.4
1996	7.9	30.7	61.4
1998	8.3	31.4	60.3
2000	8.4	31.2	60.4
2002	8.3	31.0	60.7
2004	8.5	32.0	59.5
2006	8.5	31.7	59.8
2007	8.4	31.5	60.1

Source: The Fraser Institute's Canadian Tax Simulator 2007.

Figure 5.1: Percentage of total income before tax earned, by income group, 1961–2007

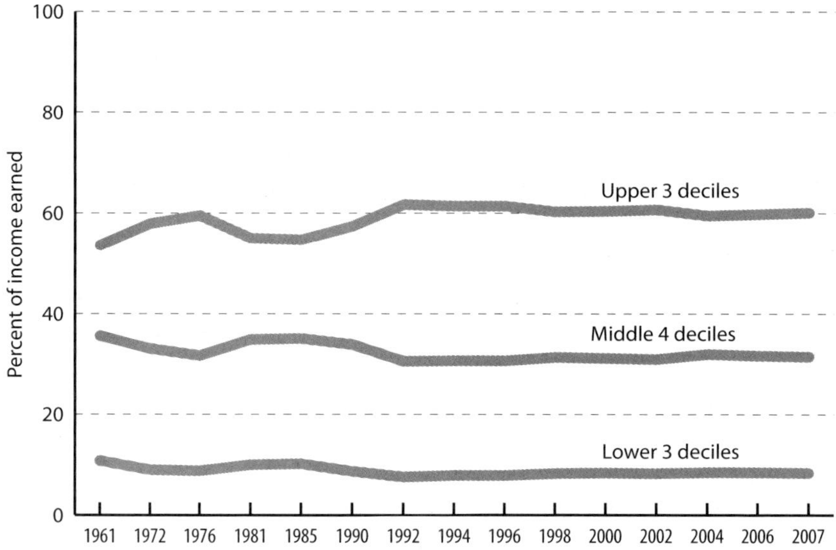

Source: The Fraser Institute's Canadian Tax Simulator 2007.

Table 5.1 reveals that the relative shares of the different income groups have been remarkably constant over the period from 1961 to 2007. A note of caution: in evaluating this result, the reader should bear in mind that a number of aspects of the data make them susceptible to misinterpretation. First, the data fail to make any allowance for the age of individuals. This is important, since age is a principal determinant of income. Young people first entering the labour market typically earn wages or salaries considerably below the average and considerably below what will be their own lifetime average. Similarly, those who have passed the age of retirement are typically in a phase of their life when their incomes are considerably below their lifetime average and when they are spending the savings and pensions accumulated from their working lifetimes.

To illustrate this point, table 5.2 displays the "life-cycle average expected wage" for a Canadian male in 2005. Three sources of data on the earnings profile are available: information from *Income Statistics* published by Canada Revenue Agency (CRA), Statistics Canada's income surveys, and Statistics Canada's Social Policy Simulation Database and Model (SPSD/M). While the three sources yield different estimates, they all show the large fluctuations in income relative to the average that one is likely to experience throughout one's life.

Failure to account for the age of income earners can lead to a considerably distorted impression of how income distribution is changing because there have been dramatic changes in the age structure of the population in

Table 5.2: Income in age groups as a percentage of average for all age groups, Canadian males, 2005

	Revenue Canada taxation statistics (%)	Statistics Canada income survey data (%)	Social Policy Simulation Database and Model (%)	Mixed profile (%)
Under 25	32.3	30.7	30.1	31.0
25–34	85.5	93.8	91.8	90.4
35–44	119.0	121.3	122.7	121.0
45–54	135.3	137.8	138.6	137.2
55–64	123.9	117.0	118.2	119.7
65 & over	83.5	79.4	77.8	80.2

Sources: Statistics Canada, *Income Trends in Canada 1980-2005*, cat. 13F0022 (CANSIM Table 202-0407); Canada and Revenue Agency, *Income Statistics, 2007 edition* (2005 Tax Year); Social Policy Simulation Database and Model (version 15.0); calculations by the authors.

Canada. Birth rates have declined and mortality rates have decreased since the 1960s (World Bank, 2007). In 1966, the ratio of Canadians under 20 to Canadians over 65 was 5.5 to 1. This ratio decreased to 1.9 by 2005, and is projected to decline further to 1.1 by the year 2021 and to 0.85 by the year 2031 (Statistics Canada, 2005). In future years, as the number of people retired or nearing retirement grows, we can expect that the distribution of income will be affected. More of the population will be elderly and more of the population will have lower incomes as a result. This will not mean, however, that the population is, in a real sense, worse off.

A second important warning for those who would draw conclusions from these data about the equity of the income distribution is that they ignore income-in-kind that people receive from government. Housing, medical care, education, and other services that are received as direct benefits from government rather than as cash payments are not reflected in the income distribution. The public provision of these services represents one of the most substantial redistributive aspects of Canadian society.

For these reasons, it would be inappropriate to infer from the data in table 5.1 that there has been no change in the effective distribution of income since 1961. The data in their present form are incapable of providing meaningful answers to that question. What the data do provide is a yardstick against which to measure the distribution of taxes. This yardstick will allow us to infer whether, for example, groups of people with low incomes bear a disproportionate share of the tax burden. It will provide an indication of the progressivity or regressivity of the Canadian tax burden. In order to arrive at these results, it is necessary to combine income results with those on tax distribution.

Tax distribution and tax rates

Our measurements of the distribution of the tax burden provide some interesting and, indeed, puzzling results. Whereas up until the mid-1970s there had been a more or less steady increase in the total tax burden borne by the upper income group, from 1976 to 1981 the share of the top group fell markedly. As table 5.3 and figure 5.2 show, in 1976, families in the top three income deciles accounted for fully 66.5% of the total tax payments. By 1981, this had fallen to 59.9% of the total, a decrease of 6.6 percentage points. The decline in the tax burden borne by the top three income deciles was nearly matched by a corresponding increase in the tax burden faced by those in the middle income deciles during this period. For example, families in the fourth to seventh income deciles, which had borne 27.3% of the total tax burden in 1976, were bearing 33.3% by 1981, an increase of 6.0 percentage points. Between

Table 5.3: Decile distribution (%) of taxes

	Income Groups Lower 3 deciles (%)	Middle 4 deciles (%)	Upper 3 deciles (%)
1961	8.7	30.6	60.9
1972	6.0	30.0	64.0
1976	6.1	27.3	66.5
1981	6.8	33.3	59.9
1985	7.1	33.6	59.4
1990	5.5	31.7	62.8
1992	4.1	27.5	68.4
1994	4.2	27.8	68.0
1996	4.2	27.9	67.9
1998	4.5	28.6	67.0
2000	4.7	28.9	66.4
2002	4.7	29.2	66.1
2004	4.9	29.7	65.4
2005	4.8	29.4	65.8
2007	4.8	29.4	65.9

Source: The Fraser Institute's Canadian Tax Simulator 2007.

Figure 5.2: Percent of total taxes paid, by income group, 1961–2007

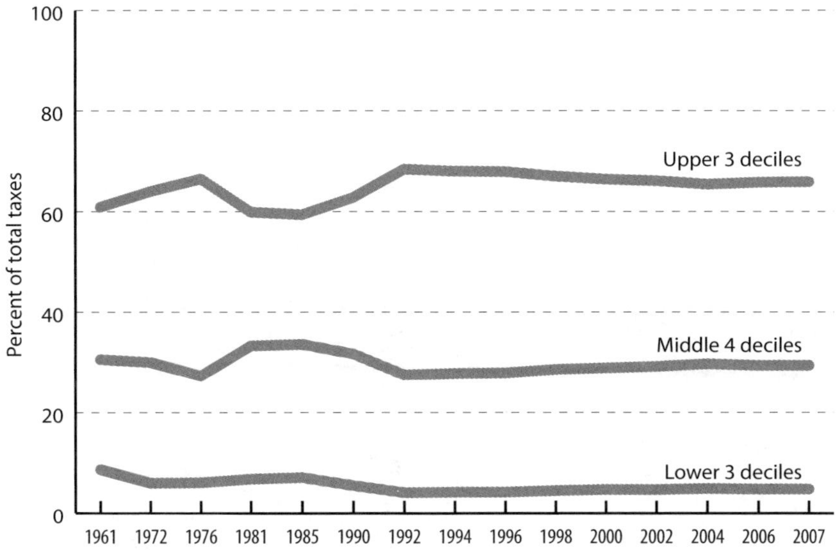

Source: The Fraser Institute's Canadian Tax Simulator 2007.

1981 and 1992, the share of the total tax burden paid by the top income group increased by 8.5 percentage points from 59.9% to 68.4% while the share paid by the middle four deciles decreased by 5.8 percentage points (33.3% to 27.5%). The trend reversed again from 1992 to 2007; during this period the total tax burden of the top 30% of income earners fell by 2.5 percentage points while the burden of the middle income group increased 1.8 percentage points.

The personal income tax paid by the upper income group (top three deciles) has increased significantly since 1985 while that paid by the lower two income groups (middle four and bottom three deciles) has been decreased. As table 5.4 shows, there had been a modest shift in the incidence of the personal income-tax system away from the upper income deciles and toward the lower income deciles until the early and mid-1980s. This was reversed in the late 1980s and early 1990s. The top three income groups accounted for 62.7% of total income tax payments in 1981, down from 68.1% in 1976. By 2007, the top three income deciles accounted for 73.2% of total income tax payments.

A major factor explaining variations in the share of taxes paid by the top three deciles has been the change in the incidence of capital-related taxes. These are chiefly property taxes and taxes on corporate profits. As table 5.5 reveals, there have been relatively large fluctuations in the pattern of these capital-related taxes. Between 1976 and 1981, the burden of taxes on

Table 5.4: Decile distribution (%) of personal income taxes

		Income Groups	
	Lower 3 deciles (%)	Middle 4 deciles (%)	Upper 3 deciles (%)
1976	3.2	29.5	68.1
1981	4.4	32.9	62.7
1985	4.5	34.3	61.2
1990	3.8	31.0	65.2
1992	2.2	23.6	74.2
1994	2.4	23.6	74.0
1996	2.4	23.5	74.1
1998	2.5	23.7	73.8
2000	2.6	24.2	73.2
2002	2.5	24.0	73.5
2004	2.5	24.7	72.8
2006	2.3	24.6	73.1
2007	2.3	24.5	73.2

Source: The Fraser Institute's Canadian Tax Simulator 2007.

profits for the top three deciles dropped from 72.2% to 66.9%. The burden crept up to 71.8% in 1985; fell to 63.1% in 1998, before increasing to 64.3% in 2000. From 2000 to 2007, the share of taxes on profits paid by the top income group decreased to 63.3%.

Table 5.5: Decile distribution (%) of profit taxes and property taxes

Profit taxes

	Income Groups		
	Lower 3 deciles (%)	Middle 4 deciles (%)	Upper 3 deciles (%)
1976	10.3	17.8	72.2
1981	9.1	24.0	66.9
1985	6.7	21.6	71.8
1990	5.8	24.5	69.7
1992	5.5	27.0	67.5
1994	5.2	26.4	68.3
1996	5.2	26.9	67.8
1998	6.2	30.7	63.1
2000	6.6	29.1	64.3
2002	6.8	30.4	62.8
2004	7.8	30.8	61.4
2006	7.2	30.3	62.5
2007	7.0	29.7	63.3

Property taxes

	Income Groups		
	Lower 3 deciles (%)	Middle 4 deciles (%)	Upper 3 deciles (%)
1976	10.3	17.8	72.2
1981	10.9	26.8	62.3
1985	6.6	21.6	71.8
1990	5.7	24.4	69.9
1992	5.3	26.5	68.2
1994	5.1	26.1	68.7
1996	5.1	26.6	68.3
1998	6.1	30.6	63.3
2000	6.5	28.9	64.6
2002	6.7	30.1	63.2
2004	7.7	30.6	61.7
2006	7.2	30.0	62.9
2007	7.0	29.4	63.6

Source: The Fraser Institute's Canadian Tax Simulator 2007.

Analysis of the underlying factors reveals that part of the reason for the dramatic shift in the incidence of capital taxes has been the change in the distribution of capital income amongst Canadians (see table 5.6). Changes in exemptions are another probable reason that capital taxes fell for the upper income deciles in the late 1970s and early 1980s, then rose in the late 1980s. For example, in the early 1980s Canadians took advantage of the tax preferences that the government inserted in the tax system to encourage the development of various sectors of the economy, such as oil exploration, rental housing, and Canadian films. The tax reform of 1987 effectively put an end to much of the tax preference game.

One factor that underlies all of the distribution series is the massive surge in the number of families in the upper income classes. In 1980, for example, only 26.1% of families had an income of $35,000 or more. By 2005, 80% of families enjoyed an income at least as large as that. While inflation has played a large role in this development, some of the increase in the number of families in the higher income groups is the result of the fact that an increasing number of families contain two income earners whose joint income pushes the family into the higher tax bracket. The implication of this increase in the number of families with two income earners for the distribution of taxation amongst families is that the upper income deciles seem to

Table 5.6: Decile distribution (%) of capital income

		Income Groups	
	Lower 3 deciles (%)	Middle 4 deciles (%)	Upper 3 deciles (%)
1976	10.3	17.8	72.2
1981	9.1	23.9	66.9
1985	6.8	22.0	71.2
1990	5.9	24.9	69.3
1992	5.5	27.0	67.5
1994	5.3	26.7	68.0
1996	5.3	27.1	67.6
1998	6.3	30.9	62.8
2000	6.7	29.3	64.0
2002	6.9	30.6	62.5
2004	7.9	31.1	61.1
2006	7.3	30.6	62.1
2007	7.2	30.0	62.8

Source: The Fraser Institute's Canadian Tax Simulator 2007.

be paying less and less tax because they are composed increasingly of individuals with lower incomes. As noted in chapter 2, two incomes totalling, say, $30,000 are taxed less in total than one income of $30,000. Since upper income families are increasingly composed of two income earners, this has put downward pressure on the average tax rate in this income range.

Consequently, from 1976 until 1985 the percentage of total income earned by the upper income groups had been steadily decreasing while the middle and lower income groups gained ground. This is quite clearly reflected in table 5.1, which shows the distribution of income by decile. Whereas in 1976 nearly 60% of all income was earned by those in the top three deciles, this had dropped to 54.7% by 1985. After rebounding to 61.7% in 1992, the income earned by the top three deciles has declined to 60.1% in 2007. One further implication of the distribution of total taxes is interesting to note: figure 5.2 shows that the decline in progressivity in the tax system that began to emerge in the late 1970s was reversed by 1985.

A look across the generations

The tables on income distribution presented above give only a snapshot of the number of Canadians who fall into various income groups at one point in time. We must look at these tables with an understanding of what they can and cannot tell us. These tables are perfectly adequate for showing that our tax system is progressive and how much current upper income groups pay versus current lower income groups. What these tables do not show is that, while there is a fairly constant proportion of the population in these income groups, the composition of these groups changes significantly from year to year. What this means is that there is not a "permanent under-class" stuck in the lower income group.

From simulations of lifetime income and taxes done for previous editions of this book, we know that the average lifetime tax rate is higher than the average tax rate from the snapshot. We also know that there is less inequality in average lifetime tax rates than suggested by the snapshot. This should come as no surprise since many young families start out in the low income group and work up to the middle or high income group. There is less inequality in the long term because many families will initially have low income and low taxes followed by middle income and middle taxes and possibly high income and high taxes as they move through their life cycles.

Evidence of just how much the composition of income groups fluctuates has been released from Statistics Canada's *Survey of Labour and Income Dynamics*. Table 5.7 shows the shifts in the position of a groups of people in the overall income distribution between 1996 and 1997. This table shows that there were 3.059 million people in the third income quintile in both 1996 and 1997, that 1.022 million who were in the third quintile in 1996 had moved up to the fourth in 1997, and that 0.759 million people dropped from the third to the second quintile between 1996 and 1997. Between 1996 and 1997,

- 66.8% of families did not change quintile
- 14.2% moved up one quintile
- 12.2% dropped one quintile
- 3.1% moved up more than one quintile
- 3.8% dropped more than one quintile.

Nearly one quarter (23%) of those families in the bottom two quintiles in 1996 were at least one quintile higher by 1997. Extending the study period from two to five years shows greater income mobility (Webber et al., 1999). The data show that, between 1996 and 1997,

- 49.1% of families did not change quintile
- 20.7% moved up one quintile
- 14.5% dropped one quintile
- 8.2% moved up more than one quintile
- 7.5% dropped more than one quintile

Of those initially in the bottom two quintiles, 45% moved up at least one quintile over the five-year period of the study.

Table 5.7: People classified by their family-income quintile in 1996 and 1997 (000's)

Income quintile in 1996	Income quintile in 1997: First (bottom)	Second	Third	Fourth	Fifth (top)
First (bottom)	4,019	903	245	110	41
Second	793	3,351	936	170	63
Third	298	759	3,059	1,022	191
Fourth	125	209	868	3,196	905
Fifth (top)	80	92	206	816	4,114

Source: Cotton et al., 1999.

Who pays the tax bill?

Table 5.3 shows that the largest portion of the tax burden ultimately settles on the higher income groups. In 2007, the top 30% of families earned 60.1% of all income in Canada and paid 65.9% of all taxes. The bottom 30% earned 8.4% of all income and paid 4.8% of all taxes. To economists these figures are nothing out of the ordinary. Our tax system is progressive. It is not surprising to find that those earning lower income pay less tax as a proportion of their income than those earning higher income. This result may, however, come as a surprise to activists and reporters who claim that the "rich" in Canada pay no taxes. As tables 5.3 and 5.4 show, the rich bear most of Canada's taxation burden.

Some critics might counter that the rich in Canada avoid taxes by holding their wealth in corporations and that corporations can avoid taxes better than individuals. We address this question in chapter 7 and present the results of a study done by the Ontario government's Fair Tax Commission, which found that corporations do pay their taxes.

Who belongs to the club of the top 30% of Canadian families? A Canadian family is included in the top 30% when its cash income exceeds $81,501. The average income in this group is $143,179.

Get it from the rich!

It is often said—and all too often believed—that the key to "social welfare" or "social justice" is the redistribution of income. That is, the state should take income from those who have more and give it to those who have less. The extreme form of this prescription is "from each according to his ability [to pay] and to each according to his need"—the rule advanced in the *Communist Manifesto* (Marx and Engels, 1848).

The preceding section's analysis of who pays the income tax reveals that, as a country, Canada already engages in significant taxation of those who are relatively well-off. It remains interesting, therefore, to inquire whether or not we could achieve a more equal distribution of the benefits of the Canadian good life by taxing more of the income of the richest Canadians.

How rich is rich?

The question that immediately arises is "How rich is rich?" At what income level should the government tax away all increases in the interest of "equitable" income distribution? Top provincial statutory income tax rates apply at incomes ranging from a low of $58,595 in Quebec to a high of $111,161 in

New Brunswick. The average of the threshold at which the top rate in province applies was $80,699 in 2007. Let us, then, for the sake of illustration, select $80,000 as the maximum income that Canadians should be allowed to earn. Under this rule, all incomes above $80,000 would be subject to a 100% rate of income tax and the proceeds would be distributed to all income earners with incomes less than $80,000.

Counting the rich

In 2005, 1,697,290 persons filed tax returns reporting an income of $80,000 or more. Note that, in this section, individual and not family incomes are the focus of the analysis. Note also that this section examines personal income tax, not the total tax burden. Total income reported by these people was $257 billion. If the government had really taxed away all income beyond $80,000, the total tax revenue in 2005 would have been $54.9 billion higher than it actually was. Redistribution of this increased tax revenue to those 21.3 million tax filers with incomes less than $80,000 would yield an average annual payment of $2,582.

Taxing the "rich" is not the source of wealth

This calculation is important because it reveals the practical impossibility of "getting it from the rich and redistributing it to the poor." A look back to table 2.6 reveals that only 7.4% of tax filers earned more than $80,000 in 2005. Those who are impatient with the speed at which the economic process improves the condition of the poorest members of society ought to reflect on the fact that the same total increase in the incomes of those earning less than $80,000 would be achieved by about a 9.7% growth in total incomes, even if it were distributed in exactly the same way as it is now. What Canada needs are more "rich" people; imposing more taxes is not the way to increase anyone's wealth.

The rags-to-riches tax burden

In the previous sections, we have shown in general terms how our progressive tax system imposes ever increasing burdens on people as they earn more income. What about an individual who started off in 1961 with meagre earnings and has since improved his economic situation markedly? What kind of message does our tax system send to this person? Table 5.8 presents the results of a tax analysis for such an individual. We assume that when he started working in 1961 he was earning $2,750 a year in cash income ($4,775 total income before tax), half the average income, and that his income grew

Table 5.8: The rags-to-riches tax burden

	Cash income ($)	Total income before tax ($)	Tax ($)	Tax as a percentage of total income before tax
1961	2,750	4,775	960	20.1
1977	10,657	17,532	4,180	23.8
1987	24,850	39,525	10,482	26.5
1997	57,944	89,105	26,285	29.5
2007	135,113	200,881	65,918	32.8
Percentage increase from 1961 to 2007				
	4,813	4,107	6,766	63.2

Source: The Fraser Institute's Canadian Tax Simulator 2007.

steadily and at such a rate that by 2007 he was earning twice the average, $135,113 a year ($200,881 total income before tax).

In 1961, this person's total income before tax of $4,775 attracted a tax bill of $960 or an average tax rate on total income of 20.1%. By 1977, the hypothetical income earner had a total income before tax of $17,532 and paid taxes of $4,180, for a tax rate of 23.8%. Finally, in 2007, when his cash income was $135,113, his total income before tax was $200,881, and his taxes paid amounted to $65,918. Thus, the average tax rate on total income before tax had risen from 20.1% to 32.8%.

Over the period of 46 years from 1961 to 2007, our hypothetical income earner experienced a 4,107% increase in total income before tax. Over the same period, his taxes paid increased by 6,766% and taxes as a percentage of total income before tax increased by 63.2%.

Marginal versus average tax rates

The tax rate that one earns on the next dollar of income is called the "marginal tax rate." It can differ dramatically from the average tax rate, which is the rate that we are most accustomed to thinking about. Table 5.9 shows both marginal and average rates for different income levels; figure 5.3 illustrates them.

It is this marginal rate that enters into people's decisions about how much to work. When someone decides whether or not to work an extra hour, she asks herself how much extra she will earn and how much extra tax she will pay. She does not consider how much tax on average she is paying because this does not reflect the true return to any extra effort she may wish

Table 5.9: Average and marginal tax rates (%) in Canada, 2007

Average tax rates (%)

Lower income groups			Middle income groups				Upper income groups		
1st	2nd	3rd	4th	5th	6th	7th	8th	9th	10th
(Income measure = cash income)									
14.6	20.9	29.8	38.0	43.8	44.8	46.0	47.2	47.9	56.9
(Income measure = total income before tax)									
11.4	15.5	20.7	24.9	28.2	29.6	30.3	31.3	32.0	35.6

Marginal tax rates (%) faced when moving from a lower to a higher decile

1 ➡ 2	2 ➡ 3	3 ➡ 4	4 ➡ 5	5 ➡ 6	6 ➡ 7	7 ➡ 8	8 ➡ 9	9 ➡ 10
(Income measure = cash income)								
26.9	53.9	70.9	67.9	49.3	51.8	52.1	50.5	67.2
(Income measure = total income before tax)								
19.1	31.9	37.5	41.4	36.0	33.7	36.1	34.5	39.2

Source: The Fraser Institute's Canadian Tax Simulator 2007.

Figure 5.3: Average and marginal tax rates, by income decile, 2007

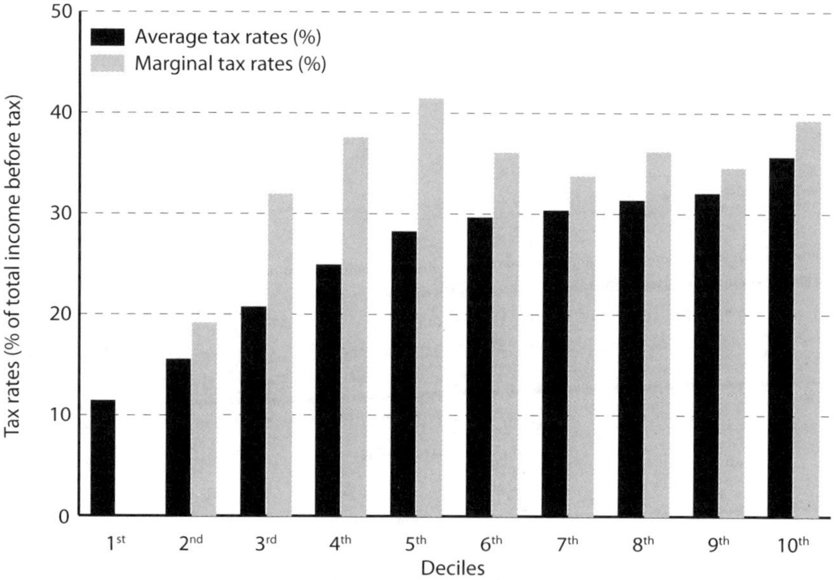

Source: The Fraser Institute's Canadian Tax Simulator 2007.

to provide. As table 5.9 shows, these rates jump considerably as one moves from the second to the third income decile, reflecting that initially it is very costly to work because one rapidly loses social assistance. The reason for this result is that many social assistance payments are reduced (the gains are "clawed back") once the recipient starts earning income. In effect, these "claw-backs" can cause the tax rate on the first few dollars of earned income to be very high. This effect fades in the middle income brackets but rises again at higher levels of income from the effect of increasing progressivity.

Chapter 6
Taxes across Canada

Taxes are the price one pays for government services. If taxes were the same in all provinces, the first five chapters of this book would be a sufficient price guide to government services. As taxes differ from province to province, however, we need to break our analysis down by province. This more detailed analysis may be of interest to Canadians who want an idea of where taxes are lightest and where they are heaviest. It may also be of interest to government officials who understand that it is dangerous for the economic health of a province when it imposes significantly more tax than its neighbours. Figure 6.1 shows the tax rate as a percentage of cash income for the average Canadian family by province.

In comparing the provinces, we must make some adjustment for the fact that the size of families differs from province to province. The family whose income is average in the province of Newfoundland & Labrador has more members than its counterpart in Ontario; Newfoundland & Labrador has relatively fewer single-member families than does Ontario. We would not be comparing the same sort of family if we set these averages side by side. To get a more precise comparison, this chapter focuses on families of two or more individuals. However, the appendix to this chapter shows that many of the results hold for families and unattached individuals, and families of two parents with two children under the age of 18.

Table 6.1 presents the tax situation for the average family by province of residence. In this context, "average family" means a family unit that has an average income in its province of residence. Thus, for example, the average

Table 6.1: Taxes of the average Canadian family (two or more individuals),

	Average cash income	Average total income before tax	Income tax	Sales tax	Amusement taxes[1]	Automobile taxes[2]
NL	64,693	129,082	9,610	5,210	2,203	1,102
PE	65,823	103,008	9,152	5,722	1,903	1,302
NS	70,031	109,372	11,224	5,491	2,232	1,039
NB	67,872	104,350	10,253	5,447	2,013	1,047
QC	72,214	111,404	11,435	5,766	1,895	863
ON	90,018	136,322	14,522	6,811	2,144	968
MB	77,604	118,754	12,239	5,684	2,563	834
SK	75,807	124,716	11,259	4,783	2,318	1,493
AB	109,052	166,376	19,029	3,304	3,740	913
BC	81,239	125,979	11,949	5,752	2,559	897
CAN	83,775	129,667	13,513	6,069	2,321	975

Note 1: Amusement taxes include liquor, tobacco, amusement, and other excise taxes.
Note 3: Payroll taxes include social security, pension, medical, and hospital taxes.
Source: The Fraser Institute's Canadian Tax Simulator 2007.

Figure 6.1: Tax rates of the average Canadian family, 2007

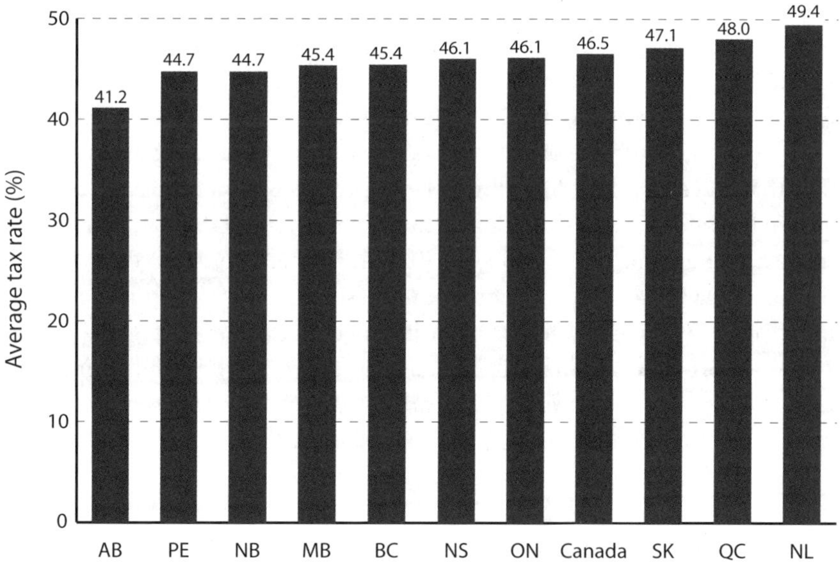

Source: The Fraser Institute's Canadian Tax Simulator 2007.

2007 (dollars)

Payroll taxes[3]	Property tax	Import duties	Profits tax	Natural resource taxes	Other taxes	Total taxes
4,968	1,404	205	3,157	3,082	1,026	31,967
5,657	2,121	215	2,701	9	622	29,405
5,508	2,032	264	3,505	595	382	32,271
5,790	2,413	241	2,376	236	512	30,329
8,035	2,510	268	3,496	(8)	429	34,688
8,842	3,321	351	3,730	24	780	41,494
5,794	2,669	278	3,253	178	1,718	35,210
5,276	3,248	268	4,077	2,008	989	35,720
7,897	1,806	394	2,563	3,770	1,464	44,881
7,294	2,595	300	2,858	1,376	1,340	36,919
8,045	2,801	317	3,440	658	853	38,992

Note 2: Automobile taxes include automobile, fuel, and motor-vehicle license taxes.

family in Newfoundland & Labrador had a cash income of $64,693 in 2007 whereas the average family in Ontario had an income of $90,018 in the same year, and so on. Table 6.2 shows which provinces have the highest propensity to tax in each of the tax categories. Income tax makes up between 30.1% and 42.4% of the family's tax bill. The highest rate is in Alberta, where the average family provides 42.4% of its taxes in income tax. The lowest proportion is in Newfoundland & Labrador, at 30.1%. The Maritimes rely most heavily upon the sales tax. For instance, 19.5¢ out of each dollar paid in taxes by the average family in Prince Edward Island are collected as sales tax. By comparison, 13.4¢ and 15.6¢ out of each tax dollar are collected as sales tax from the average family in Saskatchewan and British Columbia, while just 7.4¢ per tax dollar are collected from that source from the average Albertan family, as Alberta has no provincial sales tax. Saskatchewan has the highest reliance on property tax, collecting 9.1% of taxes in this form, whereas Alberta only collects 4.0% of its taxes as property tax.

Newfoundland & Labrador, Saskatchewan, Alberta, and British Columbia are the only provinces that have significant natural-resource revenues. In Alberta, for example, petroleum-related taxes are not collected from the tax-paying public; rather, they are collected from the corporations

Table 6.2: Individual taxes as a proportion of the total tax bill for the average

	Income tax	Sales tax	Amusement taxes[1]	Automobile taxes[2]	Payroll taxes[3]
NL	30.1	16.3	6.9	3.4	15.5
PE	31.1	19.5	6.5	4.4	19.2
NS	34.8	17.0	6.9	3.2	17.1
NB	33.8	18.0	6.6	3.5	19.1
QC	33.0	16.6	5.5	2.5	23.2
ON	35.0	16.4	5.2	2.3	21.3
MB	34.8	16.1	7.3	2.4	16.5
SK	31.5	13.4	6.5	4.2	14.8
AB	42.4	7.4	8.3	2.0	17.6
BC	32.4	15.6	6.9	2.4	19.8
CAN	34.7	15.6	6.0	2.5	20.6

Note 1: Amusement taxes include liquor, tobacco, amusement, and other excise taxes.
Note 3: Payroll taxes include social security, pension, medical, and hospital taxes.

that remove oil and gas from the ground. It is nevertheless the case that the oil and gas in the ground in Alberta belongs to the people of Alberta. Since they do not receive the income from these natural resources, it is appropriate to regard the taxes that are paid as a result of exploitation of these petroleum resources as a tax on Albertans.

While this is the appropriate technical treatment of petroleum resource taxes, apportioning these taxes in this way does confuse somewhat the inter-provincial comparison of tax burdens. If we subtracted from the $44,881 total tax bill faced by the average Albertan family the $3,770 collected on their behalf from the petroleum industry, we find that the total tax bill is reduced to $41,111 for the average family. Without natural-resource taxes, the tax bill for Newfoundland & Labrador, Saskatchewan and British Columbia would be $28,886, $33,712 and $35,543, respectively. Table 6.3 presents the ratios of taxes to income for the average family with, and without, natural-resource levies for the provinces that have significant revenues from this tax source.

In comparing the tax results for the various provinces, it is important to remember that the standard of comparison is the average family, the family in each province whose income is average. Since the average income in each province varies considerably, some of the differences in the tax burden among the provinces are due to nothing more than differences in income.

Canadian family (two or more individuals), 2007 (%)

Property tax	Import duties	Profits tax	Natural resource taxes	Other taxes
4.4	0.6	9.9	9.6	3.2
7.2	0.7	9.2	0.0	2.1
6.3	0.8	10.9	1.8	1.2
8.0	0.8	7.8	0.8	1.7
7.2	0.8	10.1	0.0	1.2
8.0	0.8	9.0	0.1	1.9
7.6	0.8	9.2	0.5	4.9
9.1	0.8	11.4	5.6	2.8
4.0	0.9	5.7	8.4	3.3
7.0	0.8	7.7	3.7	3.6
7.2	0.8	8.8	1.7	2.2

Note 2: Automobile taxes include automobile, fuel, and motor-vehicle license taxes.
Source: The Fraser Institute's Canadian Tax Simulator 2007.

Table 6.3: Ratios of taxes to cash income and to total income before taxes for an average Canadian family (two or more individuals), 2007

	Ratio (%) of taxes to cash income	Ratio (%) of taxes to total income before tax
Newfoundland and Labrador	49.4	24.8
Prince Edward Island	44.7	28.5
Nova Scotia	46.1	29.5
New Brunswick	44.7	29.1
Quebec	48.0	31.1
Ontario	46.1	30.4
Manitoba	45.4	29.6
Saskatchewan	47.1	28.6
Alberta	41.2	27.0
British Columbia	45.4	29.3
Canada	46.5	30.1
Ratios (%) excluding natural resources taxes		
Newfoundland and Labrador	44.7	22.4
Saskatchewan	44.5	27.0
Alberta	37.7	24.7
British Columbia	43.8	28.2
Canada	45.8	29.6

Source: The Fraser Institute's Canadian Tax Simulator 2007.

Table 6.4 provides a distribution of taxes by province according to income deciles. The great benefit of this table is that it makes possible a comparison of how the tax burden is distributed amongst the various income groups within each province. The outcome of this analysis, as reflected in the table, is remarkable; there is little variation among the provinces in the extent of the progressivity or regressivity of their various tax systems. The upper income groups in all provinces absorb between 62.5% and 69.2% of the total tax bill.

The similarity of the tax distributions in the provinces is noteworthy because it exists in spite of the differences in the provincial tax systems. These differences, which were pointed out above in the discussion of tables 6.1 and 6.2, ought to provide some variation in the tax rates unless, as is apparent from table 6.4, the differences in the progressivity and regressivity of the various taxes largely offset one other.

There are, however, some important differences between the tax systems in the various provinces. Table 6.5 highlights the differences in average tax rates payable by the various income deciles in each province. Thus, in New Brunswick for example, the lowest income decile paid a tax rate of 6.0% on average whereas the top decile paid a tax rate of 33.7%. In Saskatchewan, on the other hand, the bottom decile paid 14.2% while the top decile paid 32.6%.

Table 6.4: Decile distribution of taxes (%), by province, 2007

	Income Groups		
	Lower 3 deciles (%)	Middle 4 deciles (%)	Upper 3 deciles (%)
Newfoundland and Labrador	2.1	28.7	69.2
Prince Edward Island	3.6	29.7	66.8
Nova Scotia	5.2	30.2	64.6
New Brunswick	2.6	28.8	68.6
Quebec	5.2	30.6	64.2
Ontario	5.4	29.0	65.6
Manitoba	4.5	29.6	65.9
Saskatchewan	5.7	31.8	62.5
Alberta	4.5	28.3	67.3
British Columbia	3.8	29.0	67.2
Canada	4.8	29.4	65.9

Source: The Fraser Institute's Canadian Tax Simulator 2007.

Underlying this pattern of taxation is a pattern of government expenditures: the reason for raising revenues is to pay for government spending. Accordingly, an alternative, and perhaps more direct, measure of the level of government activity is the level of government spending. Table 6.6 shows both the total amounts and the per-capita amounts of provincial government spending in each of the provinces, adjusted for the amount of that spending that is financed by federal transfers to each province.

Table 6.6 reveals an interesting pattern of spending, especially when compared with the taxation data. The data reveal that Saskatchewan, Ontario, and Newfoundland & Labrador are among the provinces that spend the most and tax the most while Manitoba and the rest of the Maritime provinces, when transfer payments are removed, are among those that spend the least and tax the least.

Table 6.5: Average tax rates on total income before tax, by decile and province, 2007 (%)

	Lower income groups			Middle income groups				Upper income groups		
	1	2	3	4	5	6	7	8	9	10
NL	6.4	4.9	9.0	17.8	19.2	24.6	26.0	26.3	26.4	21.3
PE	7.7	8.5	15.8	22.3	25.3	26.5	28.2	30.6	30.0	36.0
NS	11.1	15.5	19.5	25.0	27.6	28.7	31.2	30.8	31.9	35.7
NB	6.0	6.2	13.5	18.9	23.9	28.3	29.6	30.6	31.9	33.7
QC	12.8	16.1	20.4	25.0	28.4	31.8	32.0	33.0	34.4	39.1
ON	12.6	18.3	23.5	27.0	28.6	29.8	30.6	31.4	32.7	37.5
MB	11.2	10.8	19.0	21.3	26.5	27.8	30.1	31.4	32.1	35.2
SK	14.2	14.1	18.3	22.5	26.7	27.9	30.1	30.5	31.9	32.6
AB	11.2	13.6	18.3	22.7	24.7	25.9	27.9	27.7	28.9	30.9
BC	10.2	11.8	18.8	23.9	26.4	29.2	30.1	30.8	30.6	35.3
CAN	11.4	15.5	20.7	24.9	28.2	29.6	30.3	31.3	32.0	35.6

Source: The Fraser Institute's Canadian Tax Simulator 2007.

Table 6.6: Provincial government spending, 2006/07

	Total spending ($ millions)	Amounts per person ($)			Rank by spending (net of transfers)	Rank by taxation
		Total spending	Federal transfers	Spending net of transfers		
NL	4,480	8,785	2,920	5,865	5	1
PE	1,189	8,556	3,352	5,203	9	9
NS	7,558	8,092	2,541	5,552	8	5
NB	6,580	8,786	3,213	5,573	7	8
QC[1]	54,871	7,171	1,432	5,739	6	2
ON	88,833	7,002	1,118	5,884	4	4
MB	8,800	7,471	2,622	4,848	10	7
SK	8,221	8,347	1,421	6,925	2	3
AB	29,671	8,789	914	7,875	1	10
BC	34,600	8,028	1,487	6,541	3	6

Note 1: Total provincial spending by Quebec is adjusted for abatements
Sources: Provincial budgets, 2007; Statistics Canada, Provincial Economic Accounts; The Fraser Institute; calculations by authors.

Appendix: Calculations for families and unattached individuals and for families of four consisting of two parents and two children under the age of 18

Table 6.7: Ratios (%) of taxes to cash income and to total income before taxes for families and unattached individuals, 2007

	Ratio (%) of taxes to cash income	Ratio (%) of taxes to total income before tax
Newfoundland and Labrador	47.0	22.6
Prince Edward Island	42.1	27.6
Nova Scotia	45.5	28.9
New Brunswick	42.9	28.0
Quebec	47.0	30.5
Ontario	46.0	29.9
Manitoba	42.5	27.8
Saskatchewan	45.2	27.1
Alberta	41.6	26.6
British Columbia	45.8	29.1
Canada	45.4	29.2

Note: The groups whose income is calculated in this table are the focus of chapters 3, 4, and 5.
Source: The Fraser Institute's Canadian Tax Simulator 2007.

Table: 6.8: Ratios (%) of taxes to cash income and to total income before taxes for families of four (parents and two children under 18), 2007

	Ratio (%) of taxes to cash income	Ratio (%) of taxes to total income before tax
Newfoundland and Labrador	54.3	29.3
Prince Edward Island	41.2	27.8
Nova Scotia	45.5	29.4
New Brunswick	43.3	29.4
Quebec	46.6	31.8
Ontario	43.4	30.8
Manitoba	43.5	30.3
Saskatchewan	44.6	29.0
Alberta	41.7	28.2
British Columbia	42.9	29.0
Canada	44.2	30.4

Source: The Fraser Institute's Canadian Tax Simulator 2007.

Chapter 7
Who Pays the Corporate Tax?

Corporations are a major source of revenue for federal and provincial governments. In 2006, they paid $51.4 billion in direct taxes, 10.8% of all federal and provincial government takings (tables 7.1 and 7.5). These statements are factually correct but misleading. "Corporations" do not really bear the burden of these taxes, people do. This chapter explains which people end up paying these taxes. Even though we are well furnished with data on how much corporations pay and who owns them, determining who pays the corporate tax is not straightforward. A tax on corporations is a tax on capital. When the tax rises, capital will flee and this will affect what capital and labour earn and what consumers pay. Who truly ends up bearing the tax depends on all these effects. Our calculations suggest that the elderly bear the brunt of corporate taxation.

Background on corporations and corporate tax

A corporation is a group of people bound by contract to work together and to share the rewards of that work; in its simplest terms, it is a joint venture between capitalists and workers. This description is too rudimentary to be of much help in explaining why corporations exist and to what subtle incentives they respond but it is all we need for the present discussion. Profit is what is left after labour, interest on capital, and the cost of materials have been paid, and this residual amount can be thought of as going to the people who provided the capital for the business. Corporate tax falls on profits. This is why the corporate tax is a tax on capital.

There is often confusion over what the corporate tax rate is because, as well as having their profits taxed, corporations may receive special tax breaks that allow them to write off more than their true capital expenses. This means a corporation may pay a high statutory rate on its profits but a much lower actual rate because of its deductions.

Statutory rates on capital rose in the 1970s and 1980s but revenue from the corporate tax was unsteady because profits varied and deductions had increased, eroding the tax base. It is a general principle of taxation that, if a government wants to raise a certain amount of revenue, it will distort people's choices less by imposing a low tax on a broad base than a high tax on a narrow base. By the mid-1980s, the base had become too narrow and this prompted the first stage of corporate tax reform. In the 1986 budget, the federal government started phasing out deductions such as the inventory allowance and the investment-tax credit and announced a leisurely pace at which it would reduce the statutory tax rate by 3% on average. However, tax reform in the United States lowered the corporate rate by 12% and this forced Canada to accelerate its own reforms, fearing that it would lose tax revenue to the United States because multinationals would report their revenue in the United States and their costs in Canada.

In 1987, many exemptions in the Canadian system were reduced and tax rates were decreased to 28% for large non-manufacturing firms, 23% for large manufacturing firms, and 12% for small firms. In 2007, the rates were 21% for large non-manufacturing and manufacturing firms, and 12% for small firms. The 21% rate is scheduled to decline to 19.5% in 2008, 19% in 2009, 18% in 2010, 16.5% in 2011, and 15% in 2012. The 12% rate for small firms' rate will decline to 11% in 2008. All provinces also levy corporate income tax, though at lower rates. Table 7.1 and the accompanying figure 7.1 show how federal and provincial corporate tax revenues have varied between 1961 and 2006.

Why is the corporate tax so popular?

The corporate tax has great political appeal. Ministers of finance argue convincingly that if a corporation makes profits it should pay taxes just as ordinary working people do. This argument is appealing but hides from Canadians the fact that, in the end, ordinary Canadians pay the corporate income tax. We can see this by asking what a corporation is: it is composed of machinery, contracts, office space, employees, shareholders, bondholders, and so on. These parts work together to make income for people and corporate tax is, therefore, a tax on people. The corporation itself cannot pay the tax because it is not the final destination of the income it generates. On the

Table 7.1: Corporate tax collections, 1961 to 2006 ($millions 2006)

	Provincial	Federal	Total
1961	304	1,345	1,649
1963	479	1,412	1,891
1965	545	1,652	2,197
1967	638	1,758	2,396
1969	819	2,402	3,221
1971	869	2,477	3,346
1973	1,436	3,643	5,079
1975	2,114	5,380	7,494
1977	2,103	5,135	7,238
1979	3,178	6,860	10,038
1981	3,473	9,323	12,796
1983	2,784	9,536	12,320
1985	3,977	11,586	15,563
1987	5,126	11,864	16,990
1989	6,434	12,132	18,566
1991	5,123	9,892	15,015
1993	5,568	10,695	16,263
1995	8,766	13,372	22,138
1997	12,021	20,229	32,250
1999	13,612	25,798	39,410
2001	12,129	24,223	36,352
2003	12,016	27,893	39,909
2005	15,970	33,522	49,492
2006	16,703	34,729	51,432

Sources: Statistics Canada, *National Economic and Financial Accounts*, cat. 13-001-XPB; calculations by the authors.

contrary, as the next sections show, taxes imposed on the corporation fan out to the general public by a path that is hard to trace. As J.B. Colbert said in 1665, "[t]he art of taxation consists in so plucking the goose as to obtain the largest amount of feathers with the least possible amount of hissing" (Mencken, 1989: s.v. "Taxes"). Corporate taxes cause less "hissing" than the more obvious taxes on sales or personal income. This is why politicians like the corporate tax.

Figure 7.1: Corporate tax revenue, 1961–2006 ($billions 2006)

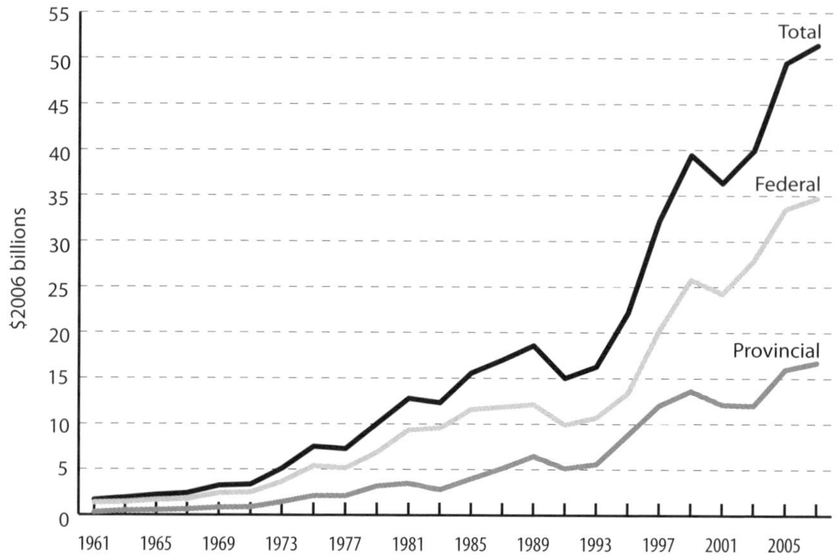

Source: Table 7.1.

Should it be so popular?

Who, in the end, pays the corporate tax? There are, of course, corporations owned by wealthy families and these families bear a portion of the tax. There are also many ordinary working people, however, who entrust their savings to mutual-fund managers. These managers invest this money in corporations and the income of those corporations flows back to these small investors. In fact, every working Canadian who earns above $3,500 indirectly owns shares in Canadian banks and many other corporations. This is because each person earning over $3,500 must contribute to the Canadian Pension Plan (CPP) and these contributions are managed by the Canada Pension Plan Investment Board, which invests the funds received in assets such as bonds and stocks to maximize returns. In addition, money set aside by employers for pensions is also invested in corporations. For example, OMERS, the Ontario Municipal Employees' Retirement System, is one of the largest stock owners and traders in Canada.

What is less obvious, but equally true, is that home-owners, farmers, cab drivers, and anyone who owns capital in the non-corporate sector of the economy also feels the impact of taxes on the corporate sector. How can this be? The reason is that capital is highly mobile. If the opportunities for making money in the corporate sector are reduced, investors will look for opportunities abroad or in the non-corporate sector—largely agriculture and real estate—at home. As investors transfer their corporate capital to this sector, capital will become more abundant there and the returns to capital there will fall. For example, those who invest in high-technology stocks may find the corporate tax gives them too little return for the risks involved and they may decide to invest their money in apartment buildings. This will add to the number of rental apartments, increase the vacancy rate, and lower the margins of profit for landlords. Thus, the tax in the corporate high-technology sector can also affect the market for commercial real estate.

This is one of many examples that show why measuring who ultimately pays the corporate tax is a difficult task. There are other factors that add to the complexity of allocating the corporate tax burden: companies can pass the tax on as higher prices or capital can leave the country, thereby making labour less productive and reducing wages.

Estimating the Canadian corporate tax

Since none of these assumptions can be dismissed out of hand, there is bound to be controversy over any estimate of who bears the corporate tax. This is why we provide several sets of calculations, each based on different, but plausible, assumptions. The main assumption we use in our calculations is that owners of capital in both corporate and non-corporate sectors bear the corporate tax but, for balance, we show what some of our results would look like if labour bore the entire tax or if it were shared between capital and labour.

Table 7.2 shows the breakdown of the corporate tax by lower-income, middle-income, and upper-income groups. As expected, the upper-income group bears most of this tax. Income deciles, however, do not tell us anything about the personal characteristics of taxpayers. A crucial question is how much of the tax various age groups pay. Table 7.3 and figure 7.2 show how much of all taxes that the government collects are paid by people of different age groups and compares this to how much corporate tax each age group pays. Even though people over 65 years of age pay little in overall taxes, they bear a disproportionate amount of the corporate tax.

These results are not surprising given our assumption that capital bears the tax. The elderly and the retired receive most of their income from capital sources such as retirement funds and rental property. For comparison, figure 7.3 shows how much different age groups would pay under the assumptions that (1) capital bears the entire tax; (2) capital and labour share the burden equally (i.e., capital and labour bear the tax in proportion to

Table 7.2: Decile distribution of profit taxes (%)

	Income groups		
	Lower 3 deciles	Middle 4 deciles	Upper 3 deciles
1976	10.3	17.8	72.2
1981	9.1	24.0	66.9
1985	6.7	21.6	71.8
1990	5.8	24.5	69.7
1992	5.5	27.0	67.5
1994	5.2	26.4	68.3
1996	5.2	26.9	67.8
1998	6.2	30.7	63.1
2000	6.6	29.1	64.3
2002	6.8	30.4	62.8
2004	7.8	30.8	61.4
2006	7.2	30.3	62.5
2007	7.0	29.7	63.3

Source: The Fraser Institute's Canadian Tax Simulator 2007.

Figure 7.2: Shares of total tax and corporate tax paid (%), by age group, 2007

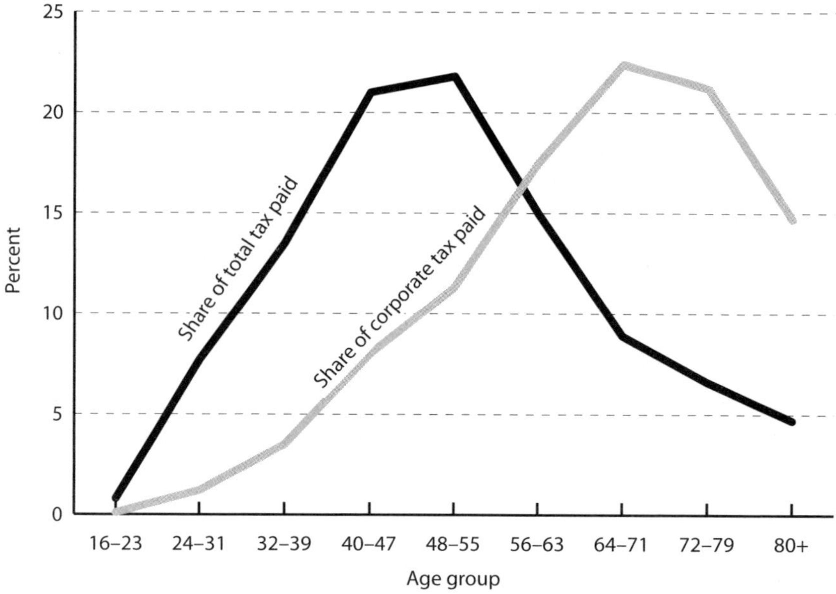

Source: The Fraser Institute's Canadian Tax Simulator 2007.

Table 7.3: Total tax and corporate tax paid, by age group, 2007

Age group	Corporate tax ($ millions)	Share of corporate tax (%)	Total tax ($ millions)	Share of total tax (%)
16–23	49	0.1	3,519	0.8
24–31	522	1.2	33,729	7.7
32–39	1,498	3.5	58,920	13.5
40–47	3,406	8.0	91,324	21.0
48–55	4,816	11.3	94,692	21.8
56–63	7,466	17.5	65,173	15.0
64–71	9,559	22.4	38,549	8.9
72–79	9,054	21.2	28,789	6.6
80+	6,246	14.7	20,635	4.7

Source: The Fraser Institute's Canadian Tax Simulator 2007.

Figure 7.3: Corporate tax as a percentage of average taxes paid in 2007, by age group, under three incidence assumptions

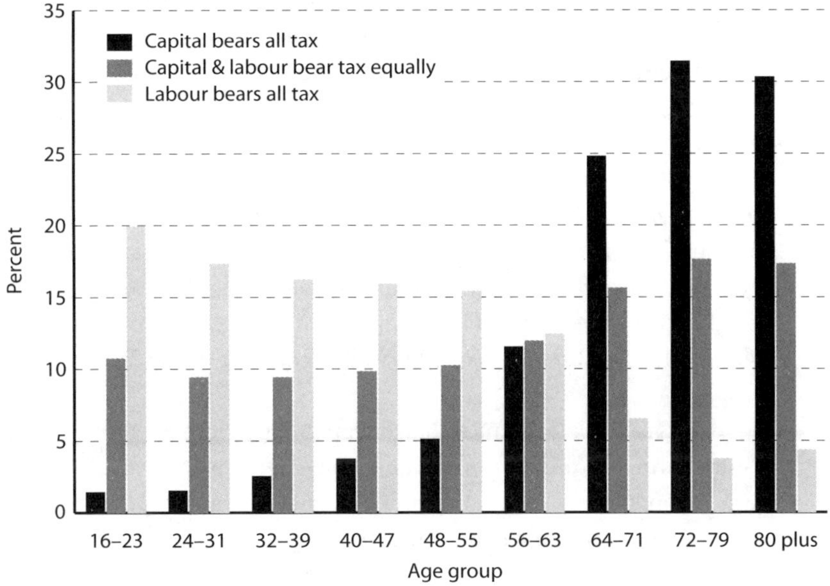

Source: The Fraser Institute's Canadian Tax Simulator 2007.

their shares in national income); (3) labour bears the entire burden. As we can see, the results are very different depending on which assumptions one makes. How reasonable each assumption is depends on what we believe about the mobility of capital between corporate and non-corporate sectors and between Canada and the rest of the world. The more mobile capital is, the less of the burden of the tax it will bear. There is an active debate over the degree to which capital can pass the tax on to labour—a debate that we cannot resolve here.[1] The point to keep in mind is that it is people who pay the corporate tax. Under two of the three possible scenarios (capital bears all, capital and labour bear equally, and labour bears all) the elderly pay significantly for a policy that is widely touted as a tax on the "rich."

The myth of the untaxed corporation

By now, it should be clear that the incidence of corporate tax is complex and that brash claims about it have to be examined cautiously. One particularly brash claim that often receives great attention from the Press is that some corporations in Canada are not paying their fair share of taxes. In particular, a labour-sponsored study claimed that 81,462 profitable corporations in Canada paid no taxes on profits of nearly $17.1 billion in 1994 and, as a result, have forced ordinary Canadians to shoulder a larger responsibility for paying the nation's taxes (British Columbia Federation of Labour, 1997).

A study by the Ontario NDP government's Fair Tax Commission shows a different picture. The Fair Tax Commission analyzed a special 1989 survey of 177,000 corporations in Ontario and reached the following conclusions:

54% OF THE PROFITS that were not taxed were inter-corporate dividends or equity income earned by subsidiaries. That is, profits earned by one branch of the corporation were transferred, after they had been taxed, to another part of the corporation. Taxing these transfers of money would be like taxing a person for moving his wallet from one pocket to another.

31% OF PROFITS were exempt either because they were used to replace depreciating equipment or because they were "paper gains," that is, assets transferred between members of the same corporate group without any economic gain or loss to the group.

1 ◆ For an extensive review of the evidence on the incidence of the corporate income tax on labour, see Gentry, 2007.

11% OF THE PROFITS not subject to tax were earned by firms that had lost money in the previous year. The tax system takes the long view of profits and allows firms to carry their losses forward. If a corporation lost $1 million last year and earned $1 million this year, over two years it has not made any profit and so should not be taxed within this two-year cycle.

4% OF PROFITS were exempt from taxation because of the temporary small-business tax holiday.

In other words, in the view of the NDP government in Ontario at the time, the survey of corporations suggested that corporations were not unfairly avoiding taxes.

Those advocating new or increased corporate taxes and claiming that corporations are getting an "easy ride" avoid statistics that show that, in recent years, corporations pay significantly more than they did in the past. Table 7.1 shows that, when we remove the effects of inflation, corporations contribute significantly more to tax revenue now than they did in the 1960s. These critics focus on the proportion of corporate taxes in total taxes collected by government, which has fallen sharply since the 1950s and 1960s. This is deceptive because, as table 7.4 shows, while corporate tax revenues as a percentage of total tax revenues have fallen by 36.8% between 1961 and 2006, corporate taxes as a share of GDP have fallen by only 11.0%. Even though governments now get a smaller fraction of their revenues from corporations than they did in 1961, this has been caused by the unprecedented growth in personal taxation that we described earlier in the book and not

Table 7.4: Importance of corporate and personal income taxes in government tax revenues

	Direct taxes as a percent of total tax revenues			Direct taxes as a percent of GDP		
	1961	2006	Change (%) 1961–2006	1961	2006	Change (%) 1961–2006
Levied on corporations	17.0	10.8	(36.8)	4.0	3.6	(11.0)
Levied on persons	23.5	36.6	56.1	5.5	12.1	119.7

Sources: Statistics Canada, National Economic and Financial Accounts; calculations by authors.

by corporations cheating the tax system. Table 7.4 also shows that direct taxes on persons as a percentage of total tax revenue increased by 56.1% from 1961 to 2006 and that direct taxes on persons as a percentage of GDP increased by 119.7%.

Yet another perspective on the claim that corporations are not paying their fair share of tax comes from the work of economist Alan Douglas (Douglas, 1990). He performed a subtle exercise to find the reasons that the corporate tax has declined as a share of total government revenue. He found that falling profits were the most significant reason for the decline: "if the profit rate for 1976 to 1985 had remained at its 1966–1975 average of 11.01% ... average [annual government] revenue would have been $11.31 billion instead of $7.55 billion. An extra $27.6 billion in corporate taxes would have been collected over the decade" (Douglas, 1990: 70).

Table 7.5: Canadian corporate taxes

	GDP ($millions)	Corporate[1] profits before taxes ($millions)	Corporate[1] profits before tax as a percentage of GDP
1961	41,253	4,498	10.9
1964	52,653	6,383	12.1
1967	69,834	7,697	11.0
1970	90,367	8,860	9.8
1973	129,196	16,888	13.1
1976	200,296	22,667	11.3
1979	280,309	38,822	13.8
1982	379,859	29,206	7.7
1985	485,714	54,665	11.3
1988	613,094	71,720	11.7
1991	685,367	38,099	5.6
1994	770,873	71,291	9.2
1997	882,733	94,585	10.7
2000	1,076,577	147,307	13.7
2003	1,213,175	157,105	12.9
2006	1,446,307	212,682	14.7

Note 1: Includes government business enterprises.
Sources: Statistics Canada, *National Economic and Financial Accounts*, Catalogue 13-001-XPB;

Table 7.5 supports this result: in almost every year shown, when corporate profits as a share of GDP increased, corporate taxes as a percent of total taxes increased. The converse is also true. Mr. Douglas found, in addition, that tax breaks, such as accelerated depreciation, reduced tax revenues much less than did declining profitability. Many of these tax breaks were eliminated in 1987 in any case. Until recently, corporations in Canada had known a long slide in profitability. Governments have not "taken it easy" on these corporations. Rather, it is simply that corporations have become a less lucrative and less reliable source of revenue than individual workers.

Corporate capital tax

The fact that taxes upon corporations' profits depend upon the relative uncertainty of corporate profits is probably the main reason for the growing popularity of taxes upon corporate capital among the provinces. In 1987,

Direct taxes from corporations[1] ($millions)	Corporate taxes as a percentage of profits	Corporate[1] tax as a percentage of total tax revenue
1,649	36.7	17.0
2,101	32.9	16.4
2,396	31.1	12.8
3,070	34.7	11.6
5,079	30.1	13.1
7,128	31.4	11.8
10,038	25.9	12.7
11,755	40.2	9.9
15,563	28.5	10.5
17,586	24.5	8.6
15,015	39.4	6.1
19,342	27.1	7.1
32,250	34.1	10.0
48,175	32.7	12.5
39,909	25.4	9.9
51,432	24.2	10.8

calculations by the authors.

four provinces imposed capital taxes on corporations and seven imposed capital taxes on banks. In 1999, only three provinces did not impose corporate capital taxes and all provinces taxed bank capital. The corporate capital tax generates revenue for the government by assessing a levy on corporations based on the amount of capital (essentially debt and equity) employed. Because it penalizes industries like software, biotechnology, and communications that make an intensive use of capital, the corporate capital tax may be the most damaging tax in Canada (Clemens et al., 2002). Fortunately, many provinces and the federal government have made a commitment to eliminating or reducing capital taxes over the course of the next few years.

Chapter 8
Canada and the Rest of the World

So far, we have concentrated our attention on how much tax Canadians pay and how those taxes have been changing. This is useful information if one wants to compare Canada today with Canada in the past. It is sufficient to concentrate on the tax burden within our own country provided one is fairly isolated from the rest of the world. However, new technology and falling trade barriers are weaving the economies of the world closer together than they have ever been before and stripping away any efforts at isolation. This means that, when we consider our taxes, we also have to look at the tax rates and levels in the countries with which we have close ties.

How do we compare?

The Canadian tax system is complex and no single number can summarize it. The same is true of comparisons between Canada and the rest of the world. Foreign tax systems are different and governments abroad provide their citizens with different levels of services. This means that comparing the total amount paid in taxes in Canada and in, say, Japan may tell us little about whether taxes are too high in one country relative to the other. For example, Canada may tax more than other countries but it may provide more and better public services. That is, the tax price of government activity may be lower here. This sort of subtlety does not mean, however, that international comparisons are meaningless. There are some numbers that can give us a broad feel for the differences among the systems.

The level of taxes

Figure 8.1 shows the total amount paid in taxes in Canada and the 29 other members of the Organisation for Economic Co-operation and Development (OECD) as a percentage of GDP in 2005. The horizontal bar for each country is divided into five sections: income and profit taxes; social-security taxes; property taxes; goods and services taxes; and other taxes. Table 8.1 shows the numerical breakdown of the relative importance of each tax category. The comparison shows that Canada ranks eleventh lowest in terms of taxes paid as a percentage of GDP. However, it collects significantly more taxes as a portion of its economy—33.4% of GDP—than neighbouring United States, where taxes absorb only 27.3% of GDP. A closer look reveals that Canada ranks among the heaviest users of income and profit taxes and property taxes. On the other hand, Canada is less reliant on social-security and goods and services taxes compared to most other countries. Some claim that these low social-security taxes give Canada room to raise contribution rates but they miss certain facts. Canada's population is comparatively young so our social-security taxes should be low. Japan has a relatively old population and social-security taxes there are over one third of the total tax bill. Contributions to the Canada Pension Plan have already increased from the 1997 rate of 6.0% to 9.9% in 2003.

Canada's overall tax burden since 1965 has been rising rapidly. Table 8.2 shows that the percentage increase in our taxes as a share of GDP from 1965 to 2005 was 30.0%. Canada's debt is a hidden tax that does not come out in this international comparison of visible taxes. Table 8.3 shows Canada's government debt as a fraction of GDP and compares it to other industrialized countries. Among the 28 OECD countries that report comparable debt statistics, fifteen have lower ratio of debt to GDP than Canada.

Why bother comparing?

Comparing taxes is interesting because it indicates how well a country can compete in the international marketplace. Taxes raise the costs facing a business and, if there is no offsetting movement in the exchange rate, they may cripple its ability to undersell foreign competitors who come from countries with lower tax burdens. We must be careful before jumping to conclusions, however, because in return for paying taxes we receive government services that help us to be productive. Infrastructures such as roads, schools, and legal and penal systems that work as they should are all vital aids to success in facing the challenge of foreign competition. This means that we have to ask whether a rapidly rising tax burden represents heavier investments

Figure 8.1: International comparison of taxes paid as a percentage of GDP, 2005

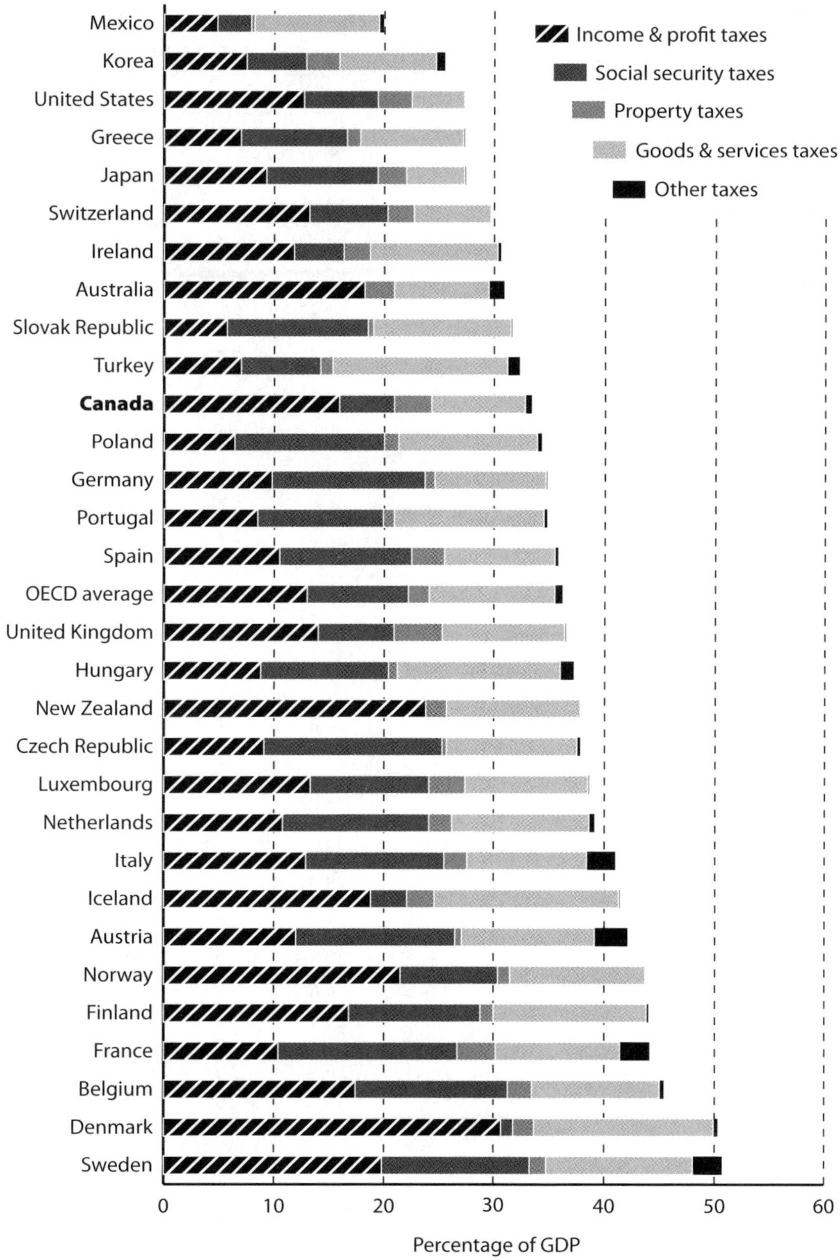

Source: Organisation for Economic Co-operation and Development (OECD), *Revenue Statistics 1965–2006*, 2007.

Table 8.1: International tax comparisons, 2005

	Total tax as a percentage of GDP	Taxes as a percent of total taxes				
		Income and profits	Social security	Property	Goods and Services	Other
Mexico	19.9	24.1	15.7	1.6	56.7	1.9
Korea	25.5	29.3	21.0	11.9	34.3	3.4
United States	27.3	46.5	24.7	11.4	17.4	0.0
Greece	27.3	25.5	35.2	4.3	34.6	0.0
Japan	27.4	33.8	36.8	9.7	19.4	0.3
Switzerland	29.7	44.5	23.9	8.0	23.6	0.0
Ireland	30.6	38.4	14.8	7.9	37.8	0.7
Australia	30.9	59.1	0.0	8.7	27.8	4.5
Slovak Republic	31.6	18.0	40.4	1.6	39.7	0.0
Turkey	32.3	21.8	22.4	3.3	49.3	3.1
Canada	**33.4**	**47.5**	**14.8**	**10.0**	**25.4**	**2.3**
Poland	34.3	18.7	39.7	3.8	36.7	0.8
Germany	34.8	28.2	39.9	2.5	29.0	0.0
Portugal	34.8	24.5	32.7	2.9	39.3	0.3
Spain	35.8	29.4	33.7	8.4	28.0	0.4
OECD average	**36.2**	**35.2**	**25.6**	**5.6**	**31.9**	**1.5**
United Kingdom	36.5	38.5	18.8	12.0	30.3	0.0
Hungary	37.2	23.6	31.3	2.3	39.7	2.9
New Zealand	37.8	63.0	0.0	4.9	32.1	0.0
Czech Republic	37.8	24.1	42.9	1.2	31.3	0.0
Luxembourg	38.6	34.4	28.0	8.5	28.8	0.1
Netherlands	39.1	27.7	33.9	5.3	31.7	0.5
Italy	41.0	31.5	30.8	5.0	26.4	5.9
Iceland	41.4	45.4	8.0	6.0	40.4	0.2
Austria	42.1	28.6	34.5	1.3	28.4	7.0
Norway	43.7	49.1	20.4	2.6	27.9	0.0
Finland	44.0	38.3	27.3	2.7	31.3	0.1
France	44.1	23.5	37.0	7.8	25.3	6.2
Belgium	45.4	38.3	30.6	4.7	25.3	0.1
Denmark	50.3	61.0	2.2	3.7	32.2	0.4
Sweden	50.7	39.1	26.7	3.0	26.1	4.8

Source: Organisation for Economic Co-operation and Development (OECD), *Revenue Statistics 1965–2006*, 2007.

Table 8.2: Change in taxes (as a percentage of GDP), 1965–2005

	Total change (%)	Change by tax type (%)			
		Income and profits	Social security	Property	Goods and Services
Australia	47.1	70.1	n/a	12.5	17.8
Austria	24.2	39.5	72.6	(53.8)	(5.5)
Belgium	46.0	102.3	41.8	83.3	(0.9)
Canada	**30.0**	**60.6**	**257.1**	**(8.1)**	**(18.3)**
Denmark	67.7	119.3	—	(20.8)	30.6
Finland	44.7	33.3	471.4	—	7.0
France	29.3	92.6	40.5	133.3	(14.5)
Germany	10.1	(8.4)	63.5	(50.0)	(2.9)
Greece	76.1	400.0	95.9	(20.0)	23.7
Iceland	58.0	235.7	57.1	150.0	1.8
Ireland	22.9	84.4	181.3	(36.8)	(11.5)
Italy	60.8	180.4	44.8	16.7	6.9
Japan	50.5	16.3	152.5	73.3	10.4
Luxembourg	39.4	34.3	21.3	94.1	60.9
Netherlands	19.2	(7.7)	31.7	50.0	31.9
New Zealand	57.5	64.1	n/a	(32.1)	80.6
Norway	47.6	66.7	154.3	22.2	—
OECD average	**42.0**	**44.4**	**100.0**	—	**18.8**
Portugal	118.9	117.9	225.7	25.0	78.9
Spain	143.5	191.7	185.7	233.3	66.7
Sweden	44.9	3.1	221.4	150.0	21.1
Switzerland	69.7	83.3	173.1	41.2	16.7
Turkey	204.7	125.8	1,100.0	—	178.9
United Kingdom	20.1	23.9	46.8	—	9.9
United States	10.5	6.7	103.0	(20.5)	(14.3)

Source: Organisation for Economic Co-operation and Development (OECD), *Revenue Statistics 1965–2006*, 2007.

Table 8.3: Net government debt as a percentage of GDP, 2007

Australia	(4.7)	Japan	88.1
Austria	36.6	Korea	(36.3)
Belgium	71.8	Luxembourg	(41.9)
Canada	**22.8**	Netherlands	30.6
Czech Republic	(5.3)	New Zealand	(11.7)
Denmark	(2.2)	Norway	(151.4)
Finland	(70.8)	Poland	16.9
France	39.2	Portugal	43.7
Germany	46.7	Slovak Republic	7.8
Greece	74.4	Spain	21.2
Hungary	54.5	Sweden	(17.7)
Iceland	5.6	Switzerland	12.9
Ireland	(0.6)	United Kingdom	39.3
Italy	90.6	United States	44.2

Source: Organisation for Economic Co-operation and Development (OECD), *OECD Economic Outlook* 82 (December), 2007.

in these productive infrastructures. It is imaginable that a higher tax burden does not represent a competitive disadvantage provided those taxes are being spent productively by government.

The evidence from 1965 to 2006 shows expenditures on these vital infrastructures as a percentage of total government spending has fallen in Canada (table 8.4). In addition, spending on the protection of persons and property, perhaps one of the most important functions of government, has declined as a percentage of total spending. A greater fraction of our tax dollar is going to finance social-service programs. These expenditures, along with interest payments on government debt, made up close to three quarters of total government spending in 2006/07.

A similar picture emerges for many of the foreign countries with which we have been comparing Canada in this chapter. Economist Vito Tanzi reports that average government spending in 17 industrialized countries rose from 27.9% to 41.5% between 1960 and 2002. The author also finds that greater spending went to social-service programs—welfare, health, education and pensions. More specifically, another study by Tanzi and Schuknecht (1995) shows that, between 1960 and 1994, average spending on interest payments in the 17 industrialized countries studied increased from 1.9% to 4.3% of GDP and average spending on subsidies and transfers

Table 8.4: Composition of total government spending, 1965/66 and 2006/07

	1965/66		2006/07		Percentage point change
	$millions	Percent of total	$millions	Percent of total	1965/66–2006/07
General services	966	5.6	19,956	3.5	(2.1)
Protection of persons & property	2,268	13.2	45,301	7.9	(5.3)
Transportation & communication	2,149	12.5	26,051	4.5	(8.0)
Health	1,678	9.8	106,850	18.6	8.8
Social services	3,112	18.1	172,374	30.0	11.9
Education	2,982	17.3	89,679	15.6	(1.7)
Resource conservation & industrial development	870	5.1	19,908	3.5	(1.6)
Environment	435	2.5	14,355	2.5	0.0
Recreation & culture	257	1.5	14,584	2.5	1.0
Labour, employment & immigration	51	0.3	2,582	0.4	0.2
Housing	23	0.1	4,782	0.8	0.7
Foreign affairs & international assistance	159	0.9	6,654	1.2	0.2
Regional planning & development	80	0.5	2,475	0.4	0.0
Research establishments	68	0.4	1,995	0.3	0.0
Transfers to own enterprises	270	1.6	n/a	n/a	n/a
Debt charges	1,718	10.0	46,107	8.0	(2.0)
Other Expenditures	122	0.7	960	0.2	(0.5)
Total expenditures	17,207	100.0	574,611	100.0	0.0

Sources: Statistics Canada, *Public Finance Historical Data, 1965/66–1991/92*, Cat. 68-512; Statistics Canada, Public Institutions Division, Financial Management System; calculations by authors.

increased from 8.3% to 23.0% of GDP. Further, Afonso, Schuknecht, and Tanzi (2005) find that small governments (public spending less than 40% of GDP) perform better than medium (public spending between 40% and 50% of GDP) or big governments (public spending greater than 50% of GDP) on a variety of different indicators: administrative, education, health and public infrastructure outcomes, income distribution, an economic stability indicator, and an economic performance indicator. What this means is that, when we are comparing tax levels, it is right to think that a higher tax burden may make a country less competitive because much of the increase in the tax burden in Canada and other industrialized countries over the past four decades is due to government activities that do not enhance the productivity of a nation.

Canada and the United States

The United States buys about 80% of Canada's exports. The proximity of the United States and the increasing flow of goods and services over our border because of NAFTA means that it is the tax system of the United States with which we ought particularly to compare our tax system. The OECD estimates that Canadian governments collected 22.3% more tax revenue (as a percentage of GDP) than their American counterparts in 2005 (OECD, 2007b). In addition, Canada collected significantly more income and profits taxes as percentage of GDP (15.9%) than the United States (12.7%).

An international comparison of business taxes

Canada's heavy reliance on income and profits taxes deserves further discussion as these types of taxes have been found to be among the most economically damaging types of taxes (Jorgenson and Yun, 1991; OECD, 1997b; Baylor and Beauséjour, 2004; Ministère des Finances du Québec, 2006). Further, a growing body of academic research has shown that business taxes discourage capital investment critical to increasing productivity and living standards (Veldhuis and Clemens, 2006). Figure 8.2 presents an international comparison of the marginal effective tax rate (METR) on capital investment, a comprehensive measure that includes income taxes, capital taxes, depreciation and inventory cost deductions, and sales taxes imposed on business inputs. Canada has one of the highest effective marginal tax rates on capital investment in the world. Specifically, Canada maintains an average METR of 30.9%, the ninth highest rate among 36 countries. Canada's METR is more than double the average rate among the 20 countries with the lowest METRs.

Figure 8.2: Marginal effective tax rates (METR) on capital investments, by country, 2007

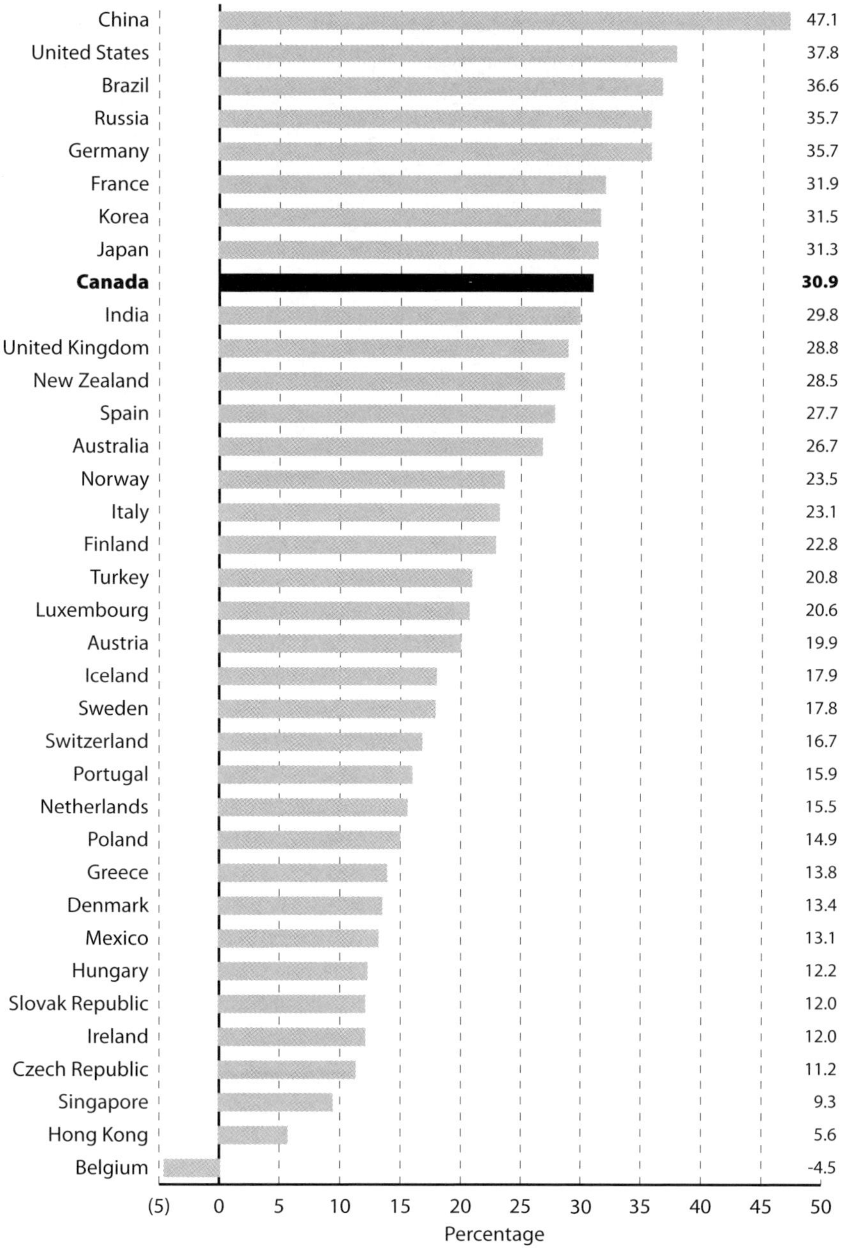

Source: Mintz, 2007.

In an effort to reduce Canada's METR, the Federal Government has committed to reduce the federal corporate income tax rate to 15% by 2012 (Canada, Department of Finance, 2007). Unfortunately, the reduction in the federal corporate income tax rate will not have a material impact on Canada's ranking internationally with respect to METRs. That is, Canada's METR will be the sixth highest among OECD countries in 2012 when the income-tax reductions are fully implemented as other countries are also reducing taxes on capital investments (Chen, 2007).

Chapter 9
Glossary of Principal Terms, Measures, and Concepts

Indices

INDEX An index is a method of measuring the percentage changes from a base year of a certain item, such as the price, volume, or value of food or the dollar amount of taxes. In order to construct an index, the price, volume, or value of the particular item being indexed in each year is divided by the price, volume, or value of the item in the base year; it is then multiplied by 100. An index has a value of 100 in the base year. In this book, the base year is 1961.

CONSUMER PRICE INDEX The Consumer Price Index measures the percentage change from a base year in the cost of purchasing a constant "basket" of goods and services representing the purchases by a particular population group in a specified time period. The Consumer Price Index (CPI) reflects price movements of some 600 items. The CPI is calculated monthly by STATISTICS CANADA (see below).

CONSUMER TAX INDEX The Consumer Tax Index measures the percentage change from a base year in the average Canadian family's tax bill. The Consumer Tax Index (CTI) is composed of federal, provincial, and municipal taxes. The CTI, calculated by the Fraser Institute, was introduced in the first edition of *Tax Facts*, which was entitled *How Much Tax Do You Really Pay?*

Statistical terms

AVERAGE CANADIAN FAMILY The average Canadian family represents a family that had average income in a particular year. The averages were constructed from Statistics Canada's expenditure and income surveys, details of which appear in the bibliography.

FAMILY A family is a group of persons dependent upon a common or pooled income for their major expenditure items and living in the same dwelling. The term also applies to a financially independent unattached individual living alone.

FAMILY EXPENDITURE SURVEY The Family Expenditure Survey refers to the surveys published by Statistics Canada that show patterns of family expenditure for Canada by selected characteristics such as urban or rural area, family type, life cycle, income, age of head, tenure, occupation of head, education of head, country of origin and year an immigrant arrived in Canada. This survey has been replaced by the SURVEY OF HOUSEHOLD SPENDING (see below).

SHELTER EXPENDITURE Shelter expenditure is included as one of the selected expenditure items in this book. It refers to expenditures on rented or owned living quarters or repairs to these quarters. Mortgage interest and payments of principal on owned living quarters and expenditures on water and heating fuel are included. The definition of shelter changed beginning in the 1997 reference year; for more information on this change, see Statistics Canada, 2002.

SOCIAL POLICY SIMULATION DATABASE AND MODEL (SPSD/M) The SPSD/M is a static microsimulation model that comprises a database, a series of tax/transfer algorithms and models, analytical software, and user documentation. The SPSD/M is a tool designed to analyze the financial interactions of governments with individuals and families in Canada. It allows estimation of the income redistributive effects or cost implications of changes in the personal taxation and cash transfer system.

STATISTICS CANADA Statistics Canada is Canada's official statistical agency, often referred to as "StatsCan." Statistics Canada provided much of the published and unpublished data for this book. For a detailed listing of these sources, see *Government sources*, in References.

SURVEY OF CONSUMER FINANCES The Survey of Consumer Finances refers to the survey from Statistics Canada that gives details of the incomes and characteristics of families. Information is given on the incomes (from, *e.g.*, salaries, wages, and pensions) of the head of family and of the spouse, residence (*e.g.*, province, rural or urban), personal characteristics (*e.g.* size of family, age and educational level of head and spouse), and labour-related characteristics (*e.g.* occupation, employment status). This survey has been replaced by the SURVEY OF LABOUR AND INCOME DYNAMICS (see below).

SURVEY OF HOUSEHOLD SPENDING (SHS) The Survey of Household Spending collects information on how much money households across the country spend on various items such as food, shelter, clothing, entertainment, transportation, health care, and other items. This survey includes households of all sizes, be it an individual or a family. The sample for this survey is over 21,000 households.

SURVEY OF LABOUR AND INCOME DYNAMICS (SLID) The Survey of Labour and Income Dynamics (SLID) is a longitudinal survey of households conducted by Statistics Canada. It is designed to capture changes in the economic well-being of individuals and families over time and the determinants of their well-being. Individuals originally selected for the survey are interviewed once or twice per year for six years to collect information about their experiences in the labour market, income, and family circumstances. In order to obtain complete information on families and to obtain cross-sectional data, people who live with the original respondents at any time during the six years are also interviewed during the time of cohabitation. The sample for this survey is approximately 30,000 households.

Income concepts

CASH INCOME Cash income is the income a family would report when completing a government survey, such as the Survey of Household Spending, the Survey of Labour and Income Dynamics, or the Census form. It includes income that one receives regularly, such as salary or wage income (before tax), and payments from government such as old age security, employment insurance, and family allowances. Families generally under-report income so the estimates of cash income used in this study are "bumped up" using a Statistics Canada adjustment to include income often omitted when a family reports its income. Often not reported are bond or bank interest and dividend income.

DECILES Deciles are a way of categorizing families. All families were arranged according to total income before tax, from lowest income to highest, and then divided into ten groups, *i.e.* the first decile contains the 10% of families with the lowest incomes, the second decile contains the 10% of families with the second lowest incomes, and so on.

HIDDEN INCOME Hidden income is income that a family receives but probably does not consider to be a part of its income. Hidden income is largely made up of employers' contributions to pension plans, medical premiums, and insurance plans. Another example is imputed non-farm rent. (For a more complete discussion of imputed non-farm rent, see the Fraser Institute's publication, *Rent Control—A Popular Paradox*, p. 33).

INCOME FROM GOVERNMENT Income from government is income that a family receives as payment from the government, whereas taxes are payments to the government. Therefore, income from the government can be considered a "negative tax." It is often referred to as a transfer payment. It includes such items as the Canada Child Tax Benefit (CCTB), old age security payments, veterans' grants, and so on.

TOTAL INCOME BEFORE TAX Total income before tax is the term used in this book to designate the amount of income the family would have received before paying tax. It is composed of cash income, which includes income from government (transfer payments), and hidden income.

TRANSFER PAYMENTS See INCOME FROM GOVERNMENT above.

Taxes

CORPORATE PROFITS TAX Corporate profits tax is the tax paid on the profits of a corporation. This is also referred to as the "corporate income tax."

DEFERRED TAXATION Deferred taxation is the debt incurred by the various levels of government to finance the expenditures that cannot be met by current tax revenue. It is, in effect, deferred taxation because the debts and the interest on them must ultimately be paid out of future tax revenue.

DIRECT TAXES Direct taxes are taxes that are paid directly by the family. Examples of direct taxes are the personal income tax and property taxes. They are often referred to as explicit taxes.

HIDDEN TAXES Hidden taxes are taxes that are concealed in the price of articles that one buys. Hidden taxes are also referred to as implicit taxes. The most well-known form of the hidden tax is the indirect tax. Examples of hidden taxes are the tobacco, fuel, and alcohol taxes and import duties.

NEGATIVE TAX See INCOME FROM GOVERNMENT above.

PROGRESSIVE, PROPORTIONAL, REGRESSIVE Progressive, proportional, and regressive are terms that refer to the proportionality of taxes on income. A tax is called proportional if it takes the same fraction of income from those with a low income as it does from those with a high income. Employment Insurance payments and Canada Pension payments up to the maximum earnings level are examples of proportional taxes. A progressive tax is one that takes a greater proportion of income from those with a high income than from those with a low income (income tax, for example). A regressive tax is one that takes a greater proportion of income from those with a low income than it does from those with a high income (sales tax, for example).

SOCIAL SECURITY TAXES Social security taxes comprise both federal and provincial taxes. The federal category includes employers' and employees' contributions to public service pensions and to Employment Insurance. Provincial social security taxes include employers' and employees' contributions to public service pensions and Workers' Compensation. Also included in this category as taxes are payments to the Canada and Quebec Pension Plans and medical and hospital insurance premiums.

TAX BURDEN The tax burden is the means of determining who ultimately pays tax and is synonymous with the term "tax incidence." Tax burden is measured by the decline in real purchasing power that results from the imposition of a tax.

POWERS OF TAXATION UNDER THE CONSTITUTION OF CANADA The general scheme of taxation in the Constitution Act, 1982 can be summarized as follows. The FEDERAL GOVERNMENT is given an unlimited power to tax. The

PROVINCIAL GOVERNMENTS are also given what amounts to an unlimited power to tax "within the province;" that is to say, an unlimited power to tax persons within their jurisdiction and to impose taxes in respect to property located, and income earned, within the province. But their taxing powers are framed in such a way as to preclude them from imposing taxes that would have the effect of creating barriers to interprovincial trade and, generally, from taxing persons and property outside the province.

References

Afonso, Antonio, Ledger Schuknecht and Vito Tanzi (2005). Public Sector Efficiency: An International Comparison. *Public Choice* 123: 321–47.

Alexander, Jared, and Joel Emes (1998). *Canadian Government Debt: A Guide to the Indebtedness of Canada and the Provinces.* Critical Issues Bulletin. Fraser Institute.

Baylor, Maximilian and Louis Beauséjour (2004). Taxation and Economic Efficiency: Results from a Canadian CGE Model. Department of Finance Working Paper. Federal Department of Finance.

Bethune, Brian A. (1993). The Competitiveness of the Canadian Tax System. *Canadian Tax Journal* 41, 6: 1119–27.

Bird, Richard M. (1970). *Growth of Government Spending in Canada.* Canadian Tax Foundation.

British Columbia Federation of Labour (1997). Corporate Tax Freedom Day. Press release (January 28).

Boucher, Michel (1998). *Évaluation de la perfomance du government du Parti québécois 1994–1998.* Communication sur des points cruciaux. Fraser Institute.

Browning, Edgar K. (1978). The Burden of Taxation. *Journal of Political Economy* 86, 4 (August): 649–71.

Browning, Edgar K., and William R. Johnson (1979). *The Distribution of the Tax Burden*. American Enterprise Institute.

Burrows, Marie. *Fiscal Positions of the Provinces: The 1983 Budgets*. Conference Board of Canada; Aeric Inc.

Campbell, Harry F. 1975). An Input-Output Analysis of the Commodity Structure of Indirect Taxes in Canada. *Canadian Journal of Economics* (August): 433.

Canadian Bankers Association (1998). *Canadian Bank Facts, 1997/98*.

Canadian Institute of Actuaries (1995). *Troubled Tomorrows: The Report of the Institute of Actuaries' Task Force on Retirement Savings* (January).

Canadian Tax Foundation (various issues). *The National Finances: An Analysis of the Revenues and Expenditures of the Government of Canada*.

Canadian Tax Foundation (various issues). *Provincial and Municipal Finances*. Canadian Tax Foundation.

Chen, Duanjie, and Kenneth J. McKenzie (1996). The Impact of Taxation on Capital Markets: An International Comparison of Effective Tax Rates on Capital. Prepared for Capital Market Issues, a conference sponsored by Industry Canada.

Chen, Duanjie (2007). Flaherty's Missed Opportunity. C.D. Howe Institute *e-brief*.

Chera, Satinder, and Fazil Mihlar (1998). *The Government of British Columbia, 1991–1998: An Assessment of Performance and a Blueprint for Economic Recovery*. Critical Issues Bulletin. Fraser Institute.

Clemens, Jason, and Joel Emes (2001). *Returning British Columbia to Prosperity*. Public Policy Sources 47. Fraser Institute.

Clemens, Jason, Joel Emes, and Rodger Scott (2002). *The Corporate Capital Tax: Canada's Most Damaging Tax*. Public Policy Sources 56. Fraser Institute.

Clemens, Jason (2002). The Big News is No News on the Corporate Capital Tax. *Fraser Forum* (November): 31–32.

Clemens, Jason, Amela Karabegovic, and Niels Veldhuis (2003). *Ontario Prosperity: Is Best of Second Best Good Enough?* Studies in Economic Prosperity 1. Fraser Institute.

Clemens, Jason, Milagros Palacios, Martin Massé, Niels Veldhuis, and Keith Godin (2007). *Canadian Provincial Investment Climate Report: 2007 Edition*. Studies in Entrepreneurship and Markets 3. Fraser Institute.

Clemens, Jason, Niels Veldhuis, and Milagros Palacios (2007). *Not All Taxes Are Created Equal*. Studies in Economic Prosperity 4. Fraser Institute.

Clemens, Jason (2008). *The Impact and Cost of Taxation in Canada: The Case for Flat Tax Reform*. Fraser Institute.

Conference Board of Canada (1996). *Provincial Outlook* 11, 2 (Spring).

Cotton, Cathy, Kevin Bishop, Phil Giles, Peter Hewer, and Yves Saint-Pierre (1999). *A Comparison of the Results of the Survey of Labour and Income Dynamics (SLID) and the Survey of Consumer Finances (SCF) 1993–1997: Update*. Catalogue no. 75F0002MIE, no. 007. Statistics Canada.

Davies, James, France St.-Hilaire, and John Whalley (1984). Some Calculations of Lifetime Tax Incidence. *American Economic Review* 74, 4 (September): 633–49.

Dodge, David A. (1975). Impact of Tax, Transfer and Expenditure Policies of Government on the Distribution of Personal Incomes in Canada. *Review of Income and Wealth* 21, 1 (March): 1–52.

Douglas, Alan V. (1990). Changes in Corporate Tax Revenue. *Canadian Tax Journal* 38, 1 (Jan./Feb): 66–81.

Emes, Joel F. (2001). January Questions and Answers. *Fraser Forum* (January): 13–15.

Emes, Joel F. (2002). April Questions and Answers. *Fraser Forum* (April): 25–26.

Esmail, Nadeem (2003). The Potential and the Penalty for Real Health Care Reform. *Fraser Forum* (October). Fraser Institute

Gentry, William (2007). *A Review of the Evidence on the Incidence of the Corporate Income Tax.* OTA Paper 101. US Department of the Treasury, Office of Tax Policy.

Gillespie, W. Irwin (1966). *Incidence of Taxes and Public Expenditures in the Canadian Economy.* Studies of the Royal Commission on Taxation 2.

Gillespie, W. Irwin (1978). *In Search of Robin Hood.* C.D. Howe Institute.

Goffman, Irving J. (1972). *The Burden of Canadian Taxation.* Tax Paper 29 (July). Canadian Tax Foundation.

Grubel, Herbert G., ed. (1998). *How to Use the Fiscal Surplus: What Is the Optimal Size of Government?* Fraser Institute.

Horry, Isabella D., and Michael A. Walker (1994). *Government Spending Facts* 2. Fraser Institute.

Jones, Laura, and Stephen Graf (2001). *Canada's Regulatory Burden.* Fraser Forum, Special Issue (August). Fraser Institute.

Jones, Laura, Tom Charette, Leanne Hachey, Shannon Martin, Pierre Emmanuel Paradis, and Robert Taylor (2005). *Rated "R": Prosperity Restricted by Red Tape.* Canadian Federation of Independent Business.

Jorgenson, Dale W. and Kun-Young Yun (1991). The Excess Burden of Taxation in the United States. *Journal of Accounting and Finances* 6: 487–508.

La Forest, G.V. (1981). *The Allocation of Taxing Power under the Canadian Constitution.* Canadian Tax Foundation.

Law, Marc T., Howard I. Markowitz, and Fazil Mihlar (1997). *The Harris Government: A Mid-term Review.* Critical Issues Bulletin. Fraser Institute.

Lewis, Perrin (1978). The Tangled Tale of Taxes and Transfers. In Michael Walker (ed.), *Canadian Confederation at the Crossroads: The Search for a Federal-Provincial Balance* (Fraser Institute): 39–105.

Marx, Karl, and Friedrich Engels (1848). *Manifesto of the Communist Party.*

Maslove, Allan M. (1972). *The Pattern of Taxation in Canada.* Economic Council of Canada (December).

McGillivray, Don (1976). An Over-Simplified Look at Our Complicated Taxes. *Financial Times of Canada* (November 8).

McInnes, Craig (1996). Revenues Go Up in Smoke after Tobacco Tax Cuts. *Globe and Mail* (August 5).

Meerman, Jacob P. (1974). The Definition of Income in Studies of Budget Incidence and Income Distribution. *Review of Income and Wealth* 20, 4 (December): 512–22.

Mencken, H.L. (1989). *A New Dictionary of Quotations on Historical Principles from Ancient and Modern Times.* Alfred A. Knopf.

Mihlar, Fazil (1998). *The Cost of Regulation in Canada, 1998 Edition.* Public Policy Sources 12. Fraser Institute.

Ministère des Finances du Québec (2006). *2005-2006 Budget: Budget Plan.* Gouvernement du Québec.

Mintz, Jack (2007). *The 2007 Tax Competitiveness Report: A Call for Comprehensive Tax Reform.* CD Howe Institute Commentary 254 (September). C.D. Howe Institute.

Murphy, Brian, Paul Roberts, and Michael Wolfson (2007). *A Profile of High-income Canadians, 1982 to 2004.* Income Research Paper Series. Catalogue no. 75F0002MIE, no. 006. Statistics Canada.

Musgrave, Richard A., and Peggy B. Musgrave (1973). *Public Finance in Theory and Practice.* McGraw-Hill.

Organisation for Economic Co-operation and Development (1997a). *Agricultural Policies, Markets and Trade: Monitoring and Outlook, 1997.* OECD.

Organisation for Economic Co-operation and Development (1997b). *OECD Economic Surveys, Canada, 1997.* OECD.

Organisation for Economic Co-operation and Development (2001). *OECD Economic Surveys, Canada, 2001.* OECD.

Organisation for Economic Co-operation and Development (2003). *OECD Economic Surveys, Canada, 2003.* OECD.

Organisation for Economic Co-operation and Development (2004). *OECD Economic Surveys, Canada, 2004.* OECD.

Organisation for Economic Co-operation and Development (2007a). *Agricultural Policies in OECD Countries, Monitoring and Evaluation, 2007.* OECD.

Organisation for Economic Co-operation and Development (2007b). *Revenue Statistics 1965–2006.* OECD.

Organisation for Economic Co-operation and Development (2007c). OECD *Economic Outlook* 82 (December). OECD.

Ort, Deborah L., and David B. Perry (2000). Provincial Budget Roundup. *Canadian Tax Journal* 48, 3: 710–33.

Pechman, Joseph A., and Benjamin A. Okner (1974). *Who Bears the Tax Burden? Studies of Government Finance.* The Brookings Institute.

Perry, David B. (1997). *Financing the Canadian Federation, 1867 to 1995: Setting the Stage for Change.* Canadian Tax Foundation.

Perry, J. Harvey (1989). *A Fiscal History of Canada—The Postwar Years.* Canadian Tax Foundation.

Schuknecht, Ludger and Vito Tanzi (2005). *Reforming Public Expenditure in Industrialised Countries: Are There Trade-Offs?* European Central Bank, Working paper series, no. 435.

Star, Spencer, and Sally C. Pipes (1976). *Income and Taxation in Canada 1961–1975.* Fraser Institute Technical Report 76–01. Fraser Institute.

Tanzi, Vito, and Ludger Schuknecht (1995). *The Growth of Government and the Reform of the State in Industrial Countries.* International Monetary Fund.

Tanzi, Vito (2005). The Economic Role of the State in the 21st Century. *Cato Journal* 25, 3 (Fall). Cato Institute.

Treff, Karin, and David B. Perry (various years). *Finances of the Nation: A Review of Expenditures and Revenues of the Federal, Provincial, and Local Governments of Canada.* Canadian Tax Foundation.

Usher, Dan (1995). *The Uneasy Case for Equalization Payments.* Fraser Institute.

Vaillancourt, Francois, Jason Clemens and Milagros Palacios (2007). *Compliance and Administrative Costs of Taxation in Canada.* In

Jason Clemens, ed., *The Impact and Cost of Taxation in Canada: The Case for a Flat Tax Reform* (Fraser Institute): 55–102.

Veldhuis, Niels, Joel Emes, Todd Fox, and Raphael Barth (2003). *Canadian Government Debt 2003: A Guide to the Indebtedness of Canada and the Provinces.* Public Policy Sources 67. Fraser Institute.

Veldhuis, Niels, and Todd Fox (2004). *Canadian Government Debt 2004: A Guide to the Indebtedness of Canada and the Provinces.* Fraser Institute Digital Publication. Fraser Institute.

Veldhuis, Niels and Jason Clemens (2006). *Productivity, Prosperity, and Business Taxes.* Studies in Economic Prosperity 3. Fraser Institute.

Walker, Michael, ed. (1976). *The Illusion of Wage and Price Control: Essays on Inflation, its Causes and its Cures.* Fraser Institute.

Walker, Michael, ed. (1978). *Canadian Confederation at the Crossroads: The Search for a Federal-Provincial Balance.* Fraser Institute.

Watkins, G. Campbell, and Michael A. Walker, eds. (1977). *Oil in the Seventies.* Fraser Institute.

Watkins, G. Campbell, and Michael A. Walker, eds. (1981). *Reaction: The National Energy Program.* Fraser Institute.

Webber, Maryanne, Cathy Cotton, Mauri Meere, Kevin Bishop, and Peter Hewer (1999). *A Comparison of the Results of the Survey of Labour and Income Dynamics (SLID) and the Survey of Consumer Finances (SCF), 1993-1996.* Statistics Canada.

Wonnacott, Ronald J., and P. Wonnacott (1967). *Free Trade between the United States and Canada.* Harvard University Press.

Wonnacott, 1975. Canada's Trade Options. Special Study for the Economic Council of Canada. Queen's Printer.

World Bank (2007). *World Development Indicators on CD-ROM, 2007.* Washington, D.C.: World Bank Publications.

World Trade Organization (2007). *Trade Policy Review, Canada, 2007*. WTO Publications.

Zelder, Martin (2000). The Ultimate Health Care Reform. *Fraser Forum* (February): 15–16.

The Fraser Institute's Series, Tax Facts

Walker, Michael, with Sally Pipes, John Raybould, and Spencer Star (1976). *How Much Tax Do You Really Pay? Your Real Tax Guide.*

Pipes, Sally, and Michael Walker (1979). *Tax Facts: The Canadian Consumer Tax Index and You.*

Pipes, Sally, and Michael Walker, with David Gill (1982). *Tax Facts 3: The Canadian Consumer Tax Index and You.*

Pipes, Sally, and Michael Walker, with Douglas Wills (1984). *Tax Facts 4: The Canadian Consumer Tax Index and You.*

Pipes, Sally, and Michael Walker, with Douglas Wills (1986). *Tax Facts 5: The Canadian Consumer Tax Index and You.*

Pipes, Sally, and Michael Walker, with Isabella Horry (1988). *Tax Facts 6: The Canadian Consumer Tax Index and You.*

Horry, Isabella, Sally Pipes, and Michael Walker (1990). *Tax Facts 7: The Canadian Consumer Tax Index and You.*

Horry, Isabella, Filip Palda, and Michael Walker (1992). *Tax Facts 8.*

Horry, Isabella, Filip Palda, and Michael Walker (1994). *Tax Facts 9.*

Horry, Isabella, Filip Palda, and Michael Walker, with Joel Emes (1997). *Tax Facts 10.*

Emes, Joel, and Michael Walker (1999). *Tax Facts 11.*

Emes, Joel, and Michael Walker (2001). *Tax Facts 12*.

Veldhuis, Niels, Joel Emes, and Michael Walker (2005). *Tax Facts 13*.

Veldhuis, Niels and Michael Walker (2006). *Tax Facts 14*.

Government sources

Bank of Canada (various issues). *Bank of Canada Review* (monthly).

Canada Revenue Agency, Income Statistics, 2007–2005 tax year. Available digitally at http://www.cra-arc.gc.ca.

Fair Tax Commission, Ontario (1992). Corporate Minimum Tax (March).

Canada, Department of Finance (1996). *The Budget Plan* (March 6).

Canada, Department of Finance (2007). *Economic Statement* (October 6).

Dominion Bureau of Statistics (1962). *Urban Family Expenditure 1962*.

Government of Canada (1867). *Constitution Act*.

Government of Canada, *House of Commons Debates* (1917). July 25: 3,765.

Industry Canada (2007). *Measuring the Costs of Red Tape for Small Business*. Briefing 2 (November). <http://www.reducingpaperburden.gc.ca>.

Natural Resources Canada (2008, January 18). *Fuel Focus* 3, 1.

Revenue Canada (1995). *Tax Statistics on Individuals, 1993 Tax Year*.

Statistics Canada (1983). *Historical Statistics of Canada*. Second Edition. Supply and Services Canada.

Statistics Canada (1992). *Public Finance Historical Data, 1965/66–1991/92*. Cat. 68-512, occasional. Public Institutions Division.

Statistics Canada (1994a). *Local Government Revenue and Expenditure*. Public Institutions Division.

Statistics Canada (1994b). *Federal Government Revenue and Expenditure*. Public Institutions Division.

Statistics Canada (1994c). *Provincial Government Revenue and Expenditure*. Public Institutions Division.

Statistics Canada (1994d). Survey of Consumer Finances. Household Surveys Division. Unpublished Data.

Statistics Canada (1995a). *Agriculture Economic Statistics*. Cat. 21-603e, annual. Supply and Services Canada.

Statistics Canada (1995b). *Income Distribution by Size in Canada*. Cat. 13-207, annual. Household Surveys Division.

Statistics Canada (1995c). *Public Sector Finance, 1994–1995*. Cat. 68-212, annual. Public Institutions Division.

Statistics Canada (1996). *Public Sector Finance, 1995–1996*. Cat. 68-212-XPB. Public Institutions Division.

Statistics Canada (2001). *Survey of Household Spending (SHS) 2001*. Custom tabulation.

Statistics Canada (2005). *Population projections for Canada, provinces and territories*. <http://www40.statcan.ca/l01/cst01/demo23c.htm>.

Statistics Canada (2006a). *Spending Patterns in Canada, 2005*. Catalogue No. 62-202-XIE.

Statistics Canada (2006b). *Survey of Household Spending (SHS) 2005*. Custom tabulation.

Statistics Canada (2007). *Income Trends in Canada 1980-2005*. CD-ROM. Cat. 13F0022-XIE.

Statistics Canada (2008). *Survey of Household Spending (SHS) 2006*. <http://www40.statcan.ca/l01/cst01/famil16a.htm>.

Statistics Canada (various issues). *Canadian Economic Observer*. Cat. 11-010-XPB.

Statistics Canada (various issues). *The Consumer Price Index*. Cat. 62-001-XPB.

Statistics Canada (various issues). *National Economic and Financial Accounts*. Cat. 13-001-XPB. Ottawa: National Accounts and Environment Division.

Statistics Canada (various issues). *National Income and Expenditure Accounts*. Cat. 13-001, Quarterly. National Accounts and Environment Division.

Statistics Canada (various issues). Public Sector Finance, Financial Management System, Public Institutions Division, Electronic data.

Statistics Canada (various issues). *Compendium of Public Sector Statistics*. Supply and Services Canada.

Statistics Canada (various issues). *Provincial Economic Accounts, Annual Estimates*. Cat. 13-213-XD. National Accounts and Environment Division.

Statistics Canada (various issues). *Public Sector Statistics*. Cat. 68-213-XIE. Public Institutions Division.

Provincial Budgets

Alberta, Ministry of Finance (2007). *Managing Our Growth, Budget 2007.*

British Columbia, Ministry of Finance (2007). *Budget and Fiscal Plan 2007/08–2009/10.*

Manitoba, Ministry of Finance (2007). *Budget 2007.*

New Brunswick, Department of Finance (2007). *Budget 2007–2008.*

Newfoundland & Labrador, Department of Finance (2007). *Budget 2007.*

Nova Scotia, Department of Finance (2007). *Budget 2007–2008.*

Ontario, Ministry of Finance (2007). *2007 Budget.*

Prince Edward Island, Department of the Provincial Treasury (2007). *Budget 2007–2008.*

Québec, Department of Finance (2007). *2007–2008 Budget.*

Saskatchewan, Ministry of Finance (2007). *Budget and Performance Plan 2007–2008.*

Publishing information

Distribution

This publication is also available from <http://www.fraserinstitute.org> in Portable Document Format (PDF) and can be read with Adobe Acrobat® or with Adobe Reader®, which is available free of charge from Adobe Systems Inc. To down-load Adobe Reader, go to this link: <http://www.adobe.com/products/acrobat/readstep2.html> with your browser. We encourage you to install the most recent version.

Ordering publications

For information about ordering the printed publications of the Fraser Institute, please contact the publications coordinator

- e-mail: sales@fraserinstitute.org
- telephone: 604.688.0221 ext. 580 or, toll free, 1.800.665.3558 ext. 580
- fax: 604.688.8539.

Media

For media enquiries, please contact our Communications Department

- telephone: 604.714.4582
- e-mail: communications@fraserinstitute.org.

Website

To learn more about the Fraser Institute and to read our publications on line, please visit our website at <http://www.fraserinstitute.org>.

Copyright

Date of issue: April 2008

Editing, design, and production: Lindsey Thomas Martin
Cover design: Bill Ray
Image for front cover: ©2008 Bill Ray

About the Fraser Institute

Our vision is a free and prosperous world where individuals benefit from greater choice, competitive markets, and personal responsibility. Our mission is to measure, study, and communicate the impact of competitive markets and government interventions on the welfare of individuals.

Founded in 1974, we are an independent research and educational organization with offices in Calgary, Montréal, Tampa, Toronto, and Vancouver, and international partners in over 70 countries. Our work is financed by tax-deductible contributions from thousands of individuals, organizations, and foundations. In order to protect its independence, the Institute does not accept grants from government or contracts for research.

關於 菲沙研究所

菲沙研究所的願景乃一自由而昌盛的世界，當中每個人得以從更豐富的選擇、具競爭性的市場及自我承擔責任而獲益。我們的使命在於量度、研究並使人知悉競爭市場及政府干預對個人福祉的影響。

創辨於1974年，我們乃一獨立的研究及教育機構，在卡加利、滿地可、坦帕、多倫多及溫哥華均設有辨事處，並在超過七十個國家擁有國際伙伴。我們的工作得到不同人仕、機構及基金透過可免稅捐獻資助。為了保持其獨立性，本研究所不接受政府的撥款或研究合約。

Sur l'Institut Fraser

Nous envisageons un monde libre et prospère, où chaque personne bénéficie d'un plus grand choix, de marchés concurrentiels et de responsabilités individuelles. Notre mission consiste à mesurer, à étudier et à communiquer l'effet des marchés concurrentiels et des interventions gouvernementales sur le bien-être des individus.

Fondé en 1974, notre Institut existe en tant qu'organisme indépendant de recherches et établissement éducatif. Nous avons des bureaux à Calgary, à Montréal, à Tampa, à Toronto, et à Vancouver, ainsi que des associés internationaux dans plus de 70 pays. Notre œuvre est financée par la contribution déductible d'impôt de milliers de personnes, d'organismes et de fondations. Pour protéger son indépendance, l'Institut Fraser n'accepte ni subvention gouvernementale ni recherche sous contrat.

Editorial Advisory Board

Supporting the Fraser Institute

For information about how to support the Fraser Institute, please contact

- Development Department, The Fraser Institute
  Fourth Floor, 1770 Burrard Street
  Vancouver, British Columbia, V6J 3G7 Canada
- telephone, toll-free: 1.800.665.3558 ext. 586
- e-mail: development@fraserinstitute.org

Calgary

- telephone: 403.216.7175 ext. 227
- fax: 403.234.9010

Montréal

- telephone: 514.281.9550 ext. 303
- fax: 514.281.9464
- e-mail: montreal@fraserinstitute.org.

Tampa, USA

- telephone: 813.961.6543
- fax: 636.773.2152
- e-mail: Joyce.Weaver@fraserinstitute.org.

Toronto

- telephone: 416.363.6575 ext. 232
- fax: 416.934.1639.

Vancouver

- telephone: 604.688.0221 ext. 586
- fax: 604.688.8539